Practical TOEIC Bridge® L&R Tests

TOEIC Bridge® L&R Tests で英語演習

Alison Kitzman

Kei Mihara

Yoshinori Tanaka

Hiroshi Kimura

Nan'un-do

**音声ファイル
無料 DL
のご案内**

このテキストの音声を無料で視聴（ストリーミング）・ダウンロードできます。自習用音声としてご活用ください。
以下のサイトにアクセスしてテキスト番号で検索してください。

https://nanun-do.com テキスト番号［ **512050** ］

※ 無線 LAN（WiFi）に接続してのご利用を推奨いたします。

※ 音声ダウンロードは Zip ファイルでの提供になります。
　 お使いの機器によっては別途ソフトウェア（アプリケーション）
　 の導入が必要となります。

はじめに

TOEIC Bridge® Listening & Reading Tests (=TOEIC Bridge® L&R Tests) は文字通り TOEIC® L&R Test への架け橋として、初中級者が英語力をチェックするのに最適です。TOEIC® L&R Test よりも易しく、100 問 1 時間で、実用的な英語コミュニケーションに必要な英語力を測ります。TOEIC Bridge® L&R Tests で基礎を固めるトレーニングを積むことで、中上級レベルにステップアップし、TOEIC® L&R Test でも高得点を取ることが期待できます。

TOEIC Bridge® L&R Tests はさまざまな形で活用されています。現在の英語力のレベルチェック、学習のモチベーションアップ、学習成果の測定などで利用されています。大学では入試の推薦資格の基準として利用したり、入学後に学生の英語力のレベルを測定したり、適切なクラスに振り分けるためのプレイスメントテストとして活用しているところもあります。

TOEIC Bridge® L&R Tests で高得点を取るためには、英語の基礎力が必要になります。リスニングと語彙・文法中心の学習を通して修得した基礎力は、単に TOEIC Bridge® L&R Tests のスコアアップだけでなく、総合的な英語力向上の原動力になります。

TOEIC Bridge® L&R Tests はリデザインされ、日常生活において効果的にコミュニケーションをとるためのベースとなる英語能力を測る出題形式になりました。それに対応して効率よく目標スコアをクリアするには、第 1 に自分の英語力にあった難易度の教材を使って学習すること、第 2 にテスト形式に慣れ、実践力を養うこと、第 3 に TOEIC Bridge® L&R Tests ならではの対策テクニックを身につけることが必要です。これらのことを念頭に置いて作成した本書は初中級レベルの学習者を対象とした教材です。

本書の特長

1. TOEIC Bridge® L&R Tests の目標スコアを 85 点（= TOEIC® L&R Test 470 点）以上に定め、着実にステップアップ
2. 各 Unit で全パートの実践練習を行うことによって解答テクニックをトレーニング
3. TOEIC Bridge® L&R Tests 頻出テーマで日常的な場面における基本表現のスキルアップ
4. TOEIC Bridge® L&R Tests 頻出単語で語彙力のグレードアップ
5. ネイティブの発音に慣れ、音読を併せて行うことでリスニング力をアップ
6. 基本的な表現や文法・用法をマスター

本書で TOEIC Bridge® L&R Tests 対策の学習を行うことによって、目標とするスコアをクリアし、総合的な英語力を向上させましょう。

2020 年春
著者

▶ TOEIC Bridge® L&R Tests とは

1. 英語力の測定　TOEIC Bridge® L&R Tests は、日常生活によくある場面や文脈の中で、実用的な コミュニケーションをとるための基礎的な英語スキルを測定します。

2. テスト形式　リスニング 50 問＋リーディング 50 問で、合計 100 問に答えるマークシート方式 のテストです。

3. 試験時間　リスニング約 25 分間＋リーディング 35 分間で、合計約 1 時間。リスニングとリーディ ングの間に休憩はありません。

4. 出題される題材　日常生活に関する場面で構成されています。
   - （外食）昼食、夕食、レストラン、予約
   - （娯楽）映画、劇、音楽、美術展、博物館
   - （住居）アパート、家、購入と賃貸、修理
   - （会社）レター、電話、E メール、オフィスでの会話
   - （買い物）食料雑貨店、衣類、ネットショッピング
   - （技術）コンピュータ、科学技術
   - （旅行）道案内、電車、航空機、タクシー、バス、船、切符、予定表、駅や空港のアナウンス、 レンタカー、ホテル、予約

5. 解答方法の指示　パートごとの解答方法の指示文は、すべて英語です。

6. 発音のスピード　リスニング問題はネイティブスピーカー（米国、オーストラリア、英国、カナダ） が発音し、ゆっくりしたスピードです。

7. 問題冊子への書き込み　解答中にメモを取ったり、問題冊子に書き込みをしたりすることはで きません。メモ書きの用紙が配布されます。

8. 問題冊子の回収　問題冊子は解答用紙と共に、試験終了時に回収されます。

9. テスト結果　スコアで表示されます。リスニングが 15 ～ 50 点、リーディングが 15 ～ 50 点で、 トータルスコアが 30 ～ 100 点（1 点刻み）で表示されます。

10. 公開テスト　年 4 回（3・6・9・11 月）実施。また独自の試験日で団体特別受験制度（IP テス ト）を実施する学校・団体・企業もあります。

▶ TOEIC Bridge® L&R Tests の出題形式

リスニングテスト（約 25 分間・50 問）

パート	問題形式	問題数	内容
Part 1	Four Pictures（画像選択問題）	6 問	句や文を聞き、4 つの絵を見て、それを最もよく表しているものを選ぶ。
Part 2	Question-Response（応答問題）	20 問	質問や発言を聞き、それに最も適切な応答を選ぶ。
Part 3	Conversations（会話問題）	10 問	2 者間の会話を聞いて、それに関する 2 つの設問に解答する。看板やお知らせなどの簡単な補足図表を参照する問題もある。
Part 4	Talks（説明文問題）	14 問	1 人の話し手による短いトークを聞いて、それに関する 2 つの設問に解答する。看板やお知らせなどの簡単な補足図表を参照する問題もある。

リーディングテスト（35 分間・50 問）

パート	問題形式	問題数	内容
Part 1	Sentence Completion（短文穴埋め問題）	15 問	語や句が 1 カ所抜けている文を読んで、それを完成させるのに最も適切な語や句を選ぶ。
Part 2	Text Completion（長文穴埋め問題）	15 問	語や句または文が 3 カ所抜けている文章を読んで、それを完成させるのに最も適切なものを選ぶ。
Part 3	Reading Comprehension（読解問題）	20 問	1 つの文書を読んで、それに関する 2 つか 3 つの設問に解答する。

▶ TOEIC Bridge® L&R Tests の学習方法

1. TOEIC Bridge® L&R Tests の出題形式に慣れ、練習問題を多く解きましょう。

2. 学校英語で学ぶ基本的な文法・用法をしっかり身につけましょう。

3. TOEIC Bridge® L&R Tests 頻出の日常生活に関する単語・熟語と併せて、実用的で簡単なビジネス単語も覚えて語彙力を増やしましょう。

4. リスニング問題攻略は音声を何度も聞き、また音読すると効果的です。

5. リーディング問題攻略は、先に設問に目を通し、問われている内容についてはゆっくり、その他の英文は速く読むようにしましょう。

本書の構成と使い方

　本書は全15ユニット。効率よく学習ができるように TOEIC Bridge® L&R Tests 頻出トピックに焦点を当て、各ユニットに全パートを配置しています。

　各ユニットは Warm-up、Test Questions、Review で構成されています。Warm-up では各ユニットのテーマに即した表現、文法や語彙をチェックします。Test Questions では実際の TOEIC Bridge® L&R Tests 形式で問題にチャレンジします。Review では各ユニットのキーワードと文法事項を確認します。

Warm-up

Check A　句や文を聞き、2枚のイラストを見て、句や文を適切に表すものを (A)(B) から選びます。

Check B　応答、会話や説明文を聞いて、質問に対する答えを聞いて読み、適切なものを (A)(B) から選びます。

Check C　短文を完成させるために、適切なものを選びます。

Test Questions

\<Listening Test\>

Part 1　Four Pictures

句や文を聞き、4つの絵を見て、句や文を最もよく表しているものを (A) 〜 (D) から1つ選びます。

Part 2　Question-Response

質問や発言を聞き、それに最も適切な応答を (A) 〜 (D) から1つ選びます。

Part 3　Conversations

2者間の短い会話を聞いて、それに関する2つの設問に最も適切な答えを (A) 〜 (D) から1つ選びます。なお、補足図表を参照する問題もあります。

Part 4　Talks

1人の話し手による短いトークを聞いて、それに関する2つの設問に最も適切な答えを (A) 〜 (D) から1つ選びます。なお、補足図表を参照する問題もあります。

\<Reading Test\>

Part 1　Sentence Completion

語や句が1カ所抜けている文を読み、それを完成させるのに最も適当なものを (A) 〜 (D) から1つ選びます。

Part 2　Text Completion

語や句または文が3カ所抜けている文章を読んで、それを完成させるのに最も適切なものを (A) 〜 (D) から1つ選びます。

Part 3　Reading Comprehension

1つの文書を読み、それに関する2つか3つの設問に対する最も適切な答えを (A) 〜 (D) から1つ選びます。

Review

A Vocabulary

語句の意味を (a) 〜 (h) から選びます。

B Grammar

空所に単語を書いて文法・用法をチェックします。

Contents

Warm-up

Check A 02

音声を聞いて英文の空所に単語を書き、適切に描写しているイラストを (A)(B) から選びなさい。

They are playing (　　　　　) in the (　　　　　).

(A)

(B)

解答 (　　)

Check B 03

音声を聞いて空所に単語を書き、質問の応答として適切なものを (A)(B) から選びなさい。

Q: Do (　　　　) have any (　　　　　　)?

(A) No, he's a famous chess player.

(B) Yes, I often go skiing in the winter.

解答 (　　)

Check C

次の英文の (　　) の中から適切なものを選びなさい。

1. She usually (go / goes) swimming on the weekend.
2. Kathy (plays / played) tennis with her friends yesterday.
3. Steve (goes / did) skiing every winter.
4. Last year, David (is / was) in Italy to play volleyball.

Useful Tips

▶画像選択問題（リスニング Part 1）
・画像選択問題は６問です。
・１つの英文や語句の音声が流れる前に４つのイラストを見て、人物が描かれている場合は、動作・状態、身に付けているもの、持ち物などをチェックしておきましょう。
・物や風景などの場合は、場所、状況、物の位置などを注意して見ておきましょう。この場合はThere is / are 構文がよく使われます。
・ネイティブの発音やスピードに慣れておきましょう。
・音声は一度しか流れないので、集中して聞きましょう。

<Listening Test>
Part 1 Four Pictures 04

As you look at the four pictures, listen to the short sentence. Choose the picture that the sentence best describes. Then mark your answer (A), (B), (C), or (D).

1. (A)  (B)

   (C)  (D)

Part 2 Question-Response 05

You will hear three questions, each followed by four possible responses. Choose the best response (A), (B), (C), or (D) to each question.

2. (A) At the local soccer club. (B) From 10 years old.
   (C) No, in 25 minutes. (D) Yes, every weekend.

3. (A) Put the ball in the box. (B) No, I played baseball.
   (C) Yes, I always do. (D) I need a new racket.

4. (A) I prefer jogging. (B) That doesn't work for me.
   (C) No, I'm afraid not. (D) Yes, I recycle my plastic.

Part 3 Conversations 06

[A] Questions 5-6 refer to the following conversation.

5. Where will the man go this weekend?
   (A) To a family event.   (B) To a sports event.
   (C) To the mountains.   (D) To the movies.

6. Who will go with the man?
   (A) His classmates.   (B) His colleagues.   (C) His family.   (D) His friends.

[B] Questions 7-8 refer to the following conversation and advertisement.

> **Why don't you learn Spanish?**
> Beginners   -   Mondays and Wednesdays
> Intermediate - Tuesdays and Thursdays
> Advanced   -   Fridays

7. According to the woman, which class would be best for the teenagers to take?
   (A) Cooking.   (B) Gardening.   (C) Karate.   (D) Spanish.

8. Look at the advertisement. When will the man's children attend the lessons if he follows the woman's advice?
   (A) Mondays and Wednesdays.   (B) Tuesdays and Thursdays.
   (C) Fridays.   (D) Any day.

Part 4 Talks 07

[A] Questions 9-10 refer to the following talk.

9. What is the speaker describing?
   (A) A board game.   (B) A lottery.
   (C) A speech contest.   (D) An exhibit.

10. According to the speaker, what did the winner use?
    (A) A white board.   (B) A microphone.   (C) Headsets.   (D) Visual aids.

[B] Questions 11-12 refer to the following talk and notice.

> **Volunteers Wanted!**
> Call the person in charge at his/her extension.
> Concerts: Bill (ext. 1507)   Contests: Jenny (ext. 1508)
> Marathons: Margaret (ext. 1607)   Parades: Michael (ext. 1608)

11. What does the speaker need?
    (A) Friendly people.   (B) Interesting activities.
    (C) Judges.   (D) Marathon runners.

12. Look at the notice. Who is most likely in charge of this event?
    (A) Bill.   (B) Jenny.   (C) Margaret.   (D) Michael.

<Reading Test>

Part 1 Sentence Completion

Questions 13-17 are incomplete sentences. Choose the word or phrase (A), (B), (C), or (D) that best completes each sentence.

13. I _____ watching all kinds of movies last month.
   - (A) enjoy
   - (B) enjoyed
   - (C) am enjoying
   - (D) have enjoyed

14. He _____ soccer with his friends every Sunday.
   - (A) play
   - (B) plays
   - (C) were played
   - (D) were playing

15. Anne _____ her hair up every time she goes to the gym.
   - (A) tie
   - (B) ties
   - (C) tied
   - (D) will tie

16. She _____ a gold medal in the Summer Olympic Games held in Rio in 2016.
   - (A) win
   - (B) wins
   - (C) won
   - (D) have won

17. It was a nice day this morning, so John _____ to go camping.
   - (A) decide
   - (B) decides
   - (C) decided
   - (D) will decide

Part 2 Text Completion

There are three numbered blanks (18), (19), and (20) in the short reading passage. Choose the answer (A), (B), (C), or (D) that best fills in the blank and completes the text.

Dear fans,

We (18)_____ to announce that today's game has been canceled due to heavy rain. The ticket you already (19)_____ will be refunded at the box office any time between 8 a.m. and 6 p.m. (20)_____

18. (A) regret
   - (B) regretted
   - (C) regretting
   - (D) will regret

19. (A) buy
   - (B) bought
   - (C) are bought
   - (D) will buy

20. (A) We want two tickets.
   - (B) We hope you enjoy the game.
   - (C) We have some great young players.
   - (D) We apologize for any inconvenience this may cause you.

Part 3 Reading Comprehension

Questions 21-22 refer to the following chat.

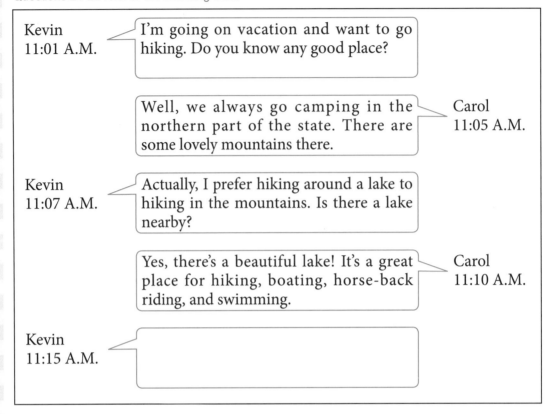

Kevin
11:01 A.M.
I'm going on vacation and want to go hiking. Do you know any good place?

Well, we always go camping in the northern part of the state. There are some lovely mountains there.
Carol
11:05 A.M.

Kevin
11:07 A.M.
Actually, I prefer hiking around a lake to hiking in the mountains. Is there a lake nearby?

Yes, there's a beautiful lake! It's a great place for hiking, boating, horse-back riding, and swimming.
Carol
11:10 A.M.

Kevin
11:15 A.M.

21. What will Kevin probably do on his holiday?
    (A) Climb a mountain
    (B) Go swimming in the hotel pool
    (C) Hike around a lake
    (D) Visit his hometown

22. Select Kevin's best response to Carol's 11:10 A.M. message.
    (A) "I'm afraid I don't have a boat."
    (B) "I don't think I can make it."
    (C) "What time shall we meet, then?"
    (D) "That sounds perfect."

Questions 23-25 refer to the following catalog.

Valley Community Center Fall Course Catalog

Registration: Aug 1-Sept 1, Online at VCCenter.gov
Yearly membership fee: Adults $50, Kids $35

Class	Time		Fee
Kids Swim & Lessons	4:00-6:00	M-F	(included in membership)
	2:00-6:00	Sat, Sun	
Spanish	7:00-8:00	T, Th	$20
Watercolor Painting	10:00-12:00	Sat	$30 + materials
Aikido	7:00-8:00	M, W, F, Sat	$25
Computer	6:00-7:00	T, Th	$30

23. How do people register for classes?

    (A) Go online   (B) By phone   (C) By mail   (D) In person

24. What is true about the Kids Swim & Lessons?

    (A) It costs extra.   (B) It's offered daily.

    (C) It's available in the morning.   (D) No instruction is included.

25. Which class is the most expensive?

    (A) Aikido   (B) Computer   (C) Spanish   (D) Watercolor Painting

Review

A Vocabulary

次の語句の意味を (a) ～ (h) から選びなさい。

1. application (   ) 2. colleague (   ) 3. describe (   ) 4. extension (   )
5. refund   (   ) 6. box office (   ) 7. in charge (   ) 8. visual aids (   )

(a) 同僚	(b) 視覚教材	(c) 内線番号	(d) チケット売り場
(e) 担当の	(f) 申し込み	(g) 払い戻す	(h) 述べる

B Grammar

次の空所に単語を書いて文法・用法を確認しなさい。

現在形

1．現在の動作・状態

We play soccer every weekend at a local 1(   ).
（私たちは毎週末、地元のクラブでサッカーをします）

Tyler lives in the suburbs of Los Angeles.
（タイラーはロサンゼルスの郊外に住んでいます）

Rosa likes to 2(   ) landscape photos as a hobby.
（ローザは趣味として風景写真を撮るのが好きです）

2．一般的な事実、ことわざ

Water boils at 100℃. （水は摂氏 100 度で沸騰します）

A rolling stone gathers no moss. （転石苔むさず）

過去形

1．過去の動作・状態

Michael hiked through the countryside yesterday.
（マイケルは昨日、田舎をハイキングしました）

Jennifer lived in Switzerland at that 3(   ).
（ジェニファーは当時、スイスに住んでいました）

I thought that he was very humble. （彼はとても謙虚だと思いました）

2．過去の反復動作

Terri went to school 4(   ) train when she was a student.
（テリは学生のとき電車で通学していました）

Eating Out

Warm-up

Check A 08

音声を聞いて英文の空所に単語を書き、適切に描写しているイラストを (A)(B) から選びなさい。

The server is taking ( ) in a ( ).

(A) (B)

解答 ( )

Check B 09

音声を聞いて空所に単語を書き、質問の応答として適切なものを (A)(B) から選びなさい。

Q: ( ) did you have ( ) at the café next door?

   (A) Last Monday, I think.

   (B) Their coffee is delicious. 解答 ( )

Check C

次の英文の ( ) の中から適切なものを選びなさい。

1. Jenny and I (had / will have) lunch together tomorrow.

2. Donna (ate / has eaten) at this restaurant many times before.

3. Our guests (has arrived / will arrive) here before tonight's party begins.

4. Jim (has worked / will work) at this café since graduating from college.

Useful Tips

▶応答問題（リスニング Part 2）
・応答問題は 20 問です。
・質問や発言を聞く前に、印刷された応答を見ておきましょう。
・質問の 5W1H (Who, When, Where, What, Why, How) に注意して聞きましょう。
・質問が疑問詞で始まる場合には、その疑問詞に対応している応答を選びます。Who なら人物、
　When なら時、Where なら場所に関するものが解答です。
・Yes/No 疑問文は、Yes や No で答えない場合もあります。
・Thank you. に対する You're welcome. などの基本的な応答パターンを覚えておきましょう。

\<Listening Test\>
Part 1 Four Pictures   10

As you look at the four pictures, listen to the short sentence. Choose the picture that the sentence best describes. Then mark your answer (A), (B), (C), or (D).

1. (A)

(B)

(C)

(D)

Part 2 Question-Response   11

You will hear three questions, each followed by four possible responses. Choose the best response (A), (B), (C), or (D) to each question.

2. (A) At the local restaurant.　(B) Can I see a menu?
   (C) From 10 a.m. to 6 p.m.　(D) That information is correct.

3. (A) She makes excellent pies.
   (B) She will probably make one on Sunday.
   (C) This pie chart is too complicated for us to understand.
   (D) They have apple pie in the cafeteria.

4. (A) Probably next week.　(B) It has a pleasant atmosphere.
   (C) I prefer chicken to fish.　(D) We open for lunch at 11:30.

Part 3 Conversations 12

[A] Questions 5-6 refer to the following conversation and menu.

> ### Menu
> Vegetarian lasagna or pizza, with fruit for dessert
> Salmon or steak, with ice cream for dessert
> Shrimp and lobster platter, with apple pie for dessert

5. What is the man going to eat?

(A) Beef.　　　(B) Lasagna.　　　(C) Seafood.　　(D) Vegetarian pizza.

6. Look at the menu. What will the woman have for dessert?

(A) Apple pie.　(B) Fruit.　　(C) Ice cream.　　(D) Shrimp and lobster.

[B] Questions 7-8 refer to the following conversation.

7. Where will the woman have dinner?

(A) At a business seminar.　　　(B) At a fast-food restaurant.

(C) At a picnic.　　　　　　　　(D) At a wedding party.

8. What will the woman do besides eating dinner?

(A) Dance.　　(B) Get married.　　(C) Play games.　　(D) Sing.

Part 4 Talks 13

[A] Questions 9-10 refer to the following talk.

9. What type of dish does the speaker explain?

(A) Appetizer.　　(B) Dessert.　　(C) Main dish.　　(D) Side dish.

10. Who most likely is the speaker?

(A) A cashier.　　(B) A concierge.　　(C) A hotel guest.　(D) A server.

[B] Questions 11-12 refer to the following talk and price list.

> ### PRICE LIST
> Cheesecake:　　$25.00
> Chiffon cake:　　$27.00
> Chocolate cake:　$28.00
> Pound cake:　　$30.00

11. What should the listener do first?

(A) Blow out the candles.　　　(B) Cut the cake.

(C) Eat the cake.　　　　　　　(D) Sing "Happy Birthday."

12. Look at the price list. How much is the cake the speaker bought?

(A) 25 dollars.　　(B) 27 dollars.　　(C) 28 dollars.　　(D) 30 dollars.

<Reading Test>
Part 1 Sentence Completion

Questions 13-17 are incomplete sentences. Choose the word or phrase (A), (B), (C), or (D) that best completes each sentence.

13. Jane _____ her friend Mari's birthday party next weekend.
    (A) attend   (B) attended   (C) has attended   (D) will attend

14. Alex _____ a vegetarian for many years now.
    (A) was   (B) has been   (C) is being   (D) will be

15. I _____ the reviews of several local restaurants on the internet later today.
    (A) will check (B) am checking   (C) checked   (D) have checked

16. George says he _____ lunch at such a fancy restaurant in his life before.
    (A) have   (B) don't have   (C) has never had (D) is having

17. Lisa _____ many friends to her restaurant since she opened it last year.
    (A) invites   (B) is inviting   (C) has invited   (D) will invite

Part 2 Text Completion

There are three numbered blanks (18), (19), and (20) in the short reading passage. Choose the answer (A), (B), (C), or (D) that best fills in the blank and completes the text.

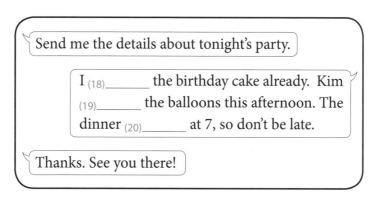

Send me the details about tonight's party.

I (18)_____ the birthday cake already. Kim (19)_____ the balloons this afternoon. The dinner (20)_____ at 7, so don't be late.

Thanks. See you there!

18. (A) am picking up
    (B) have picked up
    (C) pick up
    (D) will have picked up

19. (A) get
    (B) had gotten
    (C) has got
    (D) is going to get

20. (A) has started
    (B) start
    (C) started
    (D) starts

Part 3 Reading Comprehension

Questions 21-22 refer to the following dining facilities.

Wet Water Dining

	Time	Near	Type of food
Wee Little Lunch Box	11:30 a.m.- 3:00 p.m.	Kiddie Pool	Burgers and fries
Blizzard Mountain	11:30 a.m.- 8:00 p.m.	Wave Pool	Ice cream
Main Dining	7:00 a.m.- 9:00 p.m.	Main Entrance	Meals, salad bar
After Hours (21 and over)	5:00 p.m.-11:00 p.m.	Water Slide	Snacks, beer

21. Which of the following best describes After Hours?
    - (A) For adults only
    - (B) Near the Kiddie Pool
    - (C) Open all day
    - (D) Soft drinks only

22. Where can visitors get breakfast?
    - (A) After Hours
    - (B) Blizzard Mountain
    - (C) Main Dining
    - (D) Wee Little Lunch Box

Questions 23-25 refer to the following restaurant review.

Alice's Seafood Restaurant Review ★★★★★

 Lunch $20, Dinner $45

 Year-round outdoor patio seating

 Seafood menu, homemade desserts, vegetarian available

 A 100% smoke-free facility

 Beer, wine, cocktails, non-alcoholic mocktails

 Parking for 30 cars or motorcycles

 Adult, business casual

 11:00 a.m. to 10:00 p.m., closed Mondays

 2 party rooms for up to 40 people each, reservations required

 A full menu at alicesrestaurant.com

 Dogs on leashes allowed on patio

 423 Main Street, next to Big Super Market

23. What is the reviewer's opinion of the restaurant?
    - (A) Dinner is about $20.
    - (B) It gets five out of five stars.
    - (C) It holds 50 people.
    - (D) There's no motorcycle parking.

24. What is true about this restaurant?
    - (A) The breakfasts are popular.
    - (B) Dogs are allowed on the patio.
    - (C) It's on 4th Street.
    - (D) It's closed on holidays.

25. Besides seafood lovers, who would enjoy eating at Alice's Restaurant?
   (A) Steak lovers (B) Small children
   (C) Smokers (D) Vegetarians

Review

A Vocabulary

次の語句の意味を (a)～(h) から選びなさい。

1. appetizer (　)　2. atmosphere (　)　3. besides (　)　4. complicated (　)
5. review　 (　)　6. special　　 (　)　7. server (　)　8. banquet hall (　)

| (a) 雰囲気 | (b) 前菜 | (c) 宴会場 | (d) お勧め料理 |
| (e) 評価 | (f) 給仕 | (g) ～の他に | (h) 複雑な |

B Grammar

次の空所に単語を書いて文法・用法を確認しなさい。

未来形

1. will: 今決めたこと、不確実な未来の予測

I will make a reservation at a restaurant.（レストランの予約をします）

I will have lunch together 1(　　　) some friends.
（何人かの友だちと一緒に昼食を取ります）

2. be going to: すでに決まっている近い未来の予定

We are going to go out 2(　　　) dinner tomorrow.
（私たちは明日夕食に出かけます）

My cousin is going to arrive at the restaurant at 6:00 p.m.
（いとこはレストランに午後6時に着きます）

3. 現在形・現在進行形：未来を表現

The luncheon starts at noon. [=will start]（昼食会は正午に始まります）

What time does the party end? [=will ... end]（パーティーは何時に終わりますか）

Marie is leaving tomorrow morning. [= is going to leave]
（マリーは明日の朝、出かけます）

完了形

1. 現在完了形：現在までの完了・経験・継続 ＜have / has ＋過去分詞＞

Cathy has just got to the party.（キャシーはパーティー会場にちょうど着いたところです）

I have been to Finland before.（以前にフィンランドへ行ったことがあります）

I have eaten out three 3(　　　) in a row.（3日連続で外食しています）

2. 過去完了形：過去のある時点までの完了・経験・継続 ＜had ＋過去分詞＞

When Jim arrived at the banquet hall, the party had already started.
（ジムが宴会場に着いたとき、パーティーはすでに始まっていました）

3. 未来完了形：未来のある時点における完了・経験・継続 ＜will ＋ have ＋過去分詞＞

Betty will have finished designing the café's menu by 4(　　　) Monday.
（ベティーは来週の月曜日までにカフェのメニューをデザインすることを終えているでしょう）

Warm-up

Check A 14

音声を聞いてフレーズの空所に単語を書き、適切に描写しているイラストを (A)(B) から選びなさい。

A boy playing a (　　　　　) game on the (　　　　　).

(A)　　　　　　　　　　　　　　　　　(B)

解答 (　　)

Check B 15

音声を聞いて空所に単語を書き、質問の応答として適切なものを (A)(B) から選びなさい。

Q: (　　　　) (　　　　) is the City Museum from here?

   (A)　I'm sorry, but I cannot go with you.

   (B)　Only one kilometer, so you can easily walk there.　　解答 (　　)

Check C

次の英文の (　　) の中から適切なものを選びなさい。

1. My brother Bobby (played / is playing) a video game with his friends now.
2. (Does / Shall) we go to the museum to see the latest exhibits?
3. At the moment, Irene (watches / is watching) a movie while waiting for her mother.
4. As you are a student, you (are able / can) borrow DVDs from the library.

Useful Tips

▶会話問題（リスニング Part 3）
・会話問題は 10 問です。
・会話が流れる前に、設問と選択肢を先読みし、聞き取るべき情報をつかんでおきましょう。
・図表と関連づけて問う問題があります。会話を聞く前に図表を見ておきましょう。
・設問、選択肢、図表は問題冊子に印刷されています。
・会話がどのような場面で展開されているのか、状況を想像しながら聞きましょう。
・音声は 1 回しか流れないので、集中して内容を正確に聞き取る練習をしましょう。

<Listening Test>
Part 1 Four Pictures   16

As you look at the four pictures, listen to the phrase. Choose the picture that the phrase best describes. Then mark your answer (A), (B), (C), or (D).

1. (A)

(B)

(C)

(D)

Part 2 Question-Response   17

You will hear three questions, each followed by four possible responses. Choose the best response (A), (B), (C), or (D) to each question.

2. (A) It's going well.   (B) There are five members in the band.
   (C) The music is too loud.   (D) Twice a year, I think.

3. (A) About two and a half hours. (B) Dave is watching it now.
   (C) The theater went dark.   (D) It is now showing at several theaters.

4. (A) Five dollars for adults, two for children.
   (B) I'd love to go. It sounds like fun.
   (C) The entrance is around the corner.
   (D) You must see the science exhibition.

Part 3 Conversations 18

[A] Questions 5-6 refer to the following conversation.

5. What will the man and woman probably play?
   (A) A video game.　(B) Cards.　(C) Chess.　(D) Football.

6. What will they do in the evening?
   (A) Listen to music.　　　(A) Go see a musical.
   (C) Watch a movie.　　　(D) Watch a game.

[B] Questions 7-8 refer to the following conversation and road sign.

> **Road construction in progress!**
> Take Route 3 to get to the museums and cinema complexes.
> Take Route 5 to get to City Hall.

7. What are they going to do this weekend?
   (A) Just stay home.　　　(B) Go to an art show.
   (C) See a movie.　　　　(D) Visit City Hall.

8. Look at the road sign. What will they probably do when they see this sign?
   (A) Go back home.　(B) Go straight on.　(C) Take Route 3.　(D) Take Route 5.

Part 4 Talks 19

[A] Questions 9-10 refer to the following talk.

9. Where is this announcement most likely being made?
   (A) A concert hall.　　　(B) A movie theater.
   (C) A sports arena.　　　(D) A train station.

10. What are the listeners asked to do?
    (A) Show their tickets.　　(B) Go to their seats and sit down.
    (C) Take their shoes off.　(D) Leave their cell phones at the entrance.

[B] Questions 11-12 refer to the following talk and notice.

> *30% OFF on Mondays*
> *20% OFF on Tuesdays*
> *10% OFF on Wednesdays*

11. Which of the following best describes the Monster Coaster roller coaster?
    (A) It's world-famous.　　(B) It's not much fun to ride.
    (C) It's out of order.　　(D) It's scary fast.

12. Look at the notice. How much of a discount can visitors get today?
    (A) 10% off.　　(B) 20% off.　　(C) 30% off.　　(D) Nothing.

<Reading Test>
Part 1 Sentence Completion

Questions 13-17 are incomplete sentences. Choose the word or phrase (A), (B), (C), or (D) that best completes each sentence.

13. The concert has just ended, and the fans _____ the theater now.
    (A) are leaving   (B) was leaving   (C) has left   (D) had left

14. Instead of going to the movies, I will stay at home, since it _____ rain soon.
    (A) have to   (B) need to   (C) might   (D) ought

15. I'm sure that you _____ pass the audition, because you have practiced so hard.
    (A) might   (B) ought   (C) used to   (D) will

16. _____ you please tell me the way to the City Museum?
    (A) Could   (B) May   (C) Must   (D) Should

17. I'm afraid Billy cannot talk to you right now, because he _____ to music.
    (A) listen   (B) is listening   (C) was listening   (D) had listened

Part 2 Text Completion

There are three numbered blanks (18), (19), and (20) in the short reading passage. Choose the answer (A), (B), (C), or (D) that best fills in the blank and completes the text.

City Art Museum   *Self-Guided Tour*

Next, we will see one of Vincent van Gogh's "Sunflower" paintings (#63, oil on canvas). (18)_____ you know that he sold only one painting during his lifetime? This particular painting (19)_____ originally sold for only £12. (20)_____

---

18. (A) Did   19. (A) has
    (B) Have   (B) used to
    (C) Had   (C) was
    (D) Were   (D) would

20. (A) He could have been a famous artist.
    (B) Please hurry! The next tour is starting soon.
    (C) Today, the painting is worth millions.
    (D) Van Gogh died quite young.

Part 3 Reading Comprehension

Questions 21-22 refer to the following item.

GATEWAY ARENA	September 22 7:30 p.m.	GATEWAY ARENA	Sept 22 7:30 p.m.
	One night only! **MONA LISA** Musical Tour Live performance **ADMIT ONE**		**MONA LISA** Musical Tour $85.00
Gate: 4	Aisle: K Seat: 36	Aisle: K	Seat: 36

21. What will happen on September 22?

(A) A meeting   (B) A performance

(C) A sports event   (D) A video-game contest

22. What is this item?

(B) A bus pass   (B) A discount coupon

(C) A receipt   (D) An event ticket

Questions 23-25 refer to the following movie review.

> **MOVIE REVIEW: *Until Death Do Us Part* is a romantic comedy to die for!**
> **(Running time: 2:05 hrs)**
>
> For the second time in two years, actors John Law and Jessica Robbins team up for love and laughs. This loving couple just cannot seem to get married. Every time they start the wedding ceremony, something horrible (horribly funny, that is) stops it. Do they ever get married? Come and see!
>
> CENTRAL CINEMAS   Mon-Fri 6:00 p.m., 9:00 p.m.
> Sat and Sun 1:00 p.m., 3:15 p.m., 6:00 p.m., 9:00 p.m.

23. How long is this movie?

(A) A little over two hours   (B) Just under two hours

(C) Nearly three hours   (D) 90 minutes

24. What kind of movie is it?

(A) A drama   (B) A horror movie   (C) A love story   (D) Documentary

25. On what day can you see the movie in the early afternoon?

(A) Monday   (B) Wednesday   (C) Thursday   (D) Saturday

A Vocabulary

次の語句の意味を (a)〜(h) から選びなさい。

1. aisle 　　(　) 2. construction (　) 3. entrance (　) 4. exhibit 　　(　)

5. lifetime (　) 6. practice 　　(　) 7. City Hall (　) 8. out of order (　)

(a) 生涯	(b) 市役所	(c) 展示	(d) 入り口
(e) 通路	(f) 工事	(g) 故障して	(h) 練習する

B Grammar

次の空所に単語を書いて文法・用法の確認をしなさい。

進行形　be 動詞＋ -ing（現在分詞）

1. 現在・過去・完了・未来の進行している動作

Lucy is watching a comedy show on TV.

（ルーシーはテレビでコメディー番組を見ているところです）

When I called, Jim was playing a video game.

（電話をかけたとき、ジムはテレビゲームをしていました）

Ava has been practicing for the piano recital 1(　　　　) early this morning.

（アバは今朝早くからピアノの発表会の練習をしています）

Dave will be seeing an exhibition in an art museum tomorrow.

（デイブは明日、美術館で展示を見ているでしょう）

2. 近い未来

Brian is leaving for Sydney tonight.（ブライアンは今夜シドニーに向かう予定です）

A sightseeing bus is departing in ten 2(　　　　　　).（観光バスは 10 分後に発車します）

助動詞

1. will「〜でしょう」can「〜できる」may「〜してもよい」must「〜しなければならない」
　　should「〜すべきだ、〜のはずだ」

You should enjoy 3(　　　　　　) to tonight's rap music performance.

（あなたは今夜のラップミュージックの公演を聴くことを楽しむはずです）

We must get our movie tickets at the box office.

（私たちはチケット売り場で映画のチケットを買わなければなりません）

George will have to go to the concert hall right away.

（ジョージはすぐにコンサート会場に行かなければならないでしょう）

2. ought to「〜すべきだ」、used to「以前は〜だった」

Eric ought to invite Beth 4(　　　) the play.（エリックはベスを劇に誘うべきです）

There used to be a luxury movie theater here.

（以前ここに豪華な映画館がありました）

Warm-up

Check A   20

音声を聞いて英文の空所に単語を書き、適切に描写しているイラストを (A)(B) から選びなさい。

The plane is (　　　　　) off from the (　　　　　).

(A)
(B)

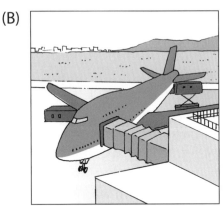

解答（　　）

Check B   21

音声を聞いて空所に単語を書き、質問の応答として適切なものを (A)(B) から選びなさい。

Q: (　　　　　) should I (　　　　　) for more flight information?

(A) The airport staff will help you.
(B) Your flight leaves from Gate 10.

解答（　　）

Check C

次の英文の（　　　）の中から適切なものを選びなさい。

1. All passengers (ask / are asked) to wait for Gate 17 to open.

2. This hotel (is known / knew) as the most luxurious hotel in this city.

3. Our parents (got / made) us go to bed early due to our early departure the next day.

4. I will get my itinerary (arrange / arranged) as soon as possible.

Useful Tips

▶説明文問題（リスニング Part 4）
・説明文問題は 14 問です。
・設問、選択肢、図表は問題冊紙に印刷されています。
・説明文が流れる前に、設問と選択肢を先読みし、聞き取るべき情報をつかんでおきましょう。
・図表と関連づけて問う問題があります。説明文を聞く前に図表を見ておきましょう。
・説明文がどのような場面でなされているのか、状況を想像しながら聞きましょう。
・音声は 1 回しか流れないので、集中して内容を正確に聞き取る練習をしましょう。

Test Questions

<Listening Test>
Part 1 Four Pictures 22

As you look at the four pictures, listen to the short sentence. Choose the picture that the sentence best describes. Then mark your answer (A), (B), (C), or (D).

1. (A)

(B)

(C)

(D)

Part 2 Question-Response 23

You will hear three questions, each followed by four possible responses. Choose the best response (A), (B), (C), or (D) to each question.

2. (A) It's yellow and black.
   (C) It's over there.
   (B) Someone forgot it.
   (D) It's John's.

3. (A) I couldn't make a reservation.
   (C) Go to the front desk.
   (B) The concierge.
   (D) In the coffee shop.

4. (A) My brother says he will come.
   (C) I will probably take a bus.
   (B) Platform Six is on the left.
   (D) The train arrives at seven.

Part 3 Conversations 24

[A] Questions 5-6 refer to the following conversation.

5. When will the next bus arrive?
   (A) In exactly 5 minutes.   (B) In only 15 minutes.
   (C) In 50 minutes.   (D) An hour from now.

6. Who most likely is the man?
   (A) A bus driver.   (B) A taxi driver.
   (C) A train conductor.   (D) An airplane pilot.

[B] Questions 7-8 refer to the following conversation and message.

Methods of payment
A house conveniently located downtown — Credit card
A house in the suburbs   — E-wallet
A house near the river   — Cash only

7. Where will they be staying?
   (A) In a fancy hotel.   (B) In someone's house.
   (C) In the heart of the city.   (D) On the beach.

8. Look at the message. How will they pay?
   (A) By e-wallet.   (B) By credit card.
   (C) Online.   (D) In cash.

Part 4 Talks 25

[A] Questions 9-10 refer to the following talk.

9. What is this flight's destination?
   (A) Boston.   (B) New York City.   (C) Seattle.   (D) Washington, D. C.

10. What is true about the plane?
    (A) It's delayed.   (B) It's the last flight today.
    (C) The gate number has changed. (D) There is little space on it for bags.

[B] Questions 11-12 refer to the following talk and schedule.

9:00 a.m. Start the tour at Central Station
9:30 a.m. Walk in the city center, shopping, lunch
2:00 p.m. Visit the old castle

11. Who is the speaker?
    (A) A flight attendant. (B) A tour guide. (C) A bus driver. (D) A passenger.

12. Look at the schedule. Where are they now ?
    (A) At Central Station.   (B) At the local café.
    (C) In the city center.   (D) In the old castle.

\<Reading Test\>
Part 1 Sentence Completion

Questions 13-17 are incomplete sentences. Choose the word or phrase (A), (B), (C), or (D) that best completes each sentence.

13. A tourism tradeshow _____ every year at this convention center.
    (A) held   (B) is held   (C) is holding   (D) will held

14. All arriving passengers _____ to fill out this card.
    (A) require   (B) required   (C) are requiring   (D) are required

15. All guest rooms _____ by our cleaning staff every day.
    (A) cleaned   (B) are cleaning   (C) are cleaned   (D) was cleaning

16. Breakfast _____ to hotel guests in the dining room.
    (A) served   (B) are served   (C) is served   (D) is serving

17. I will _____ Mr. Adams to repair my suitcase before I go on my trip.
    (A) get   (B) have   (C) let   (D) make

Part 2 Text Completion

There are three numbered blanks (18), (19), and (20) in the short reading passage. Choose the answer (A), (B), (C), or (D) that best fills in the blank and completes the text.

Ride the Historic River Liner

Enjoy a 3-day trip on our luxury train, which (18)_____ operation in 1930. Every comfort of home (19)_____ by our professional staff. We will even (20)_____ one of our porters carry all your heavy luggage.

18. (A) start
    (B) started
    (C) has started
    (D) had been started

19. (A) provides
    (B) provided
    (C) is provided
    (D) are providing

20. (A) be
    (B) can
    (C) do
    (D) have

Part 3 Reading Comprehension

Questions 21-22 refer to the following tour.

Euro Tour Day 4, Saturday

Vienna, Austria
    Temp: 75° F   Chance of Rain: 85%   Language: German   Currency: Euro

Today's Tours:	City Center Bus Tour	2.5 hours	(included)
	Palace Tour	3.5 hours	(optional, $10)
	Waltz Lesson	3 hours	(optional, $25)
	Mozart Concert	1.5 hours	(optional, $50)

---

21. What will the weather most likely be in Vienna today?
    (A) Cloudy   (B) Humid   (C) Rainy   (D) Sunny

22. Which part of the tour has already been paid for?
    (A) City Center Bus Tour   (B) Waltz Lesson
    (C) Mozart Concert   (D) Palace Tour

Questions 23-25 refer to the following notice.

TODAY! LIFEBOAT DRILL

There will be a mandatory lifeboat drill at 3:00 p.m. before we set sail.

- Your assembly station is on your keycard.
- Announcements will be made on the loudspeakers and on television displays.
- The drill will last 30 minutes after everyone has assembled.
- All onboard services will be closed from 2:30 to 3:45.

---

23. Which of the following best describes the drill?
    (A) It's on land.   (B) It's required.
    (C) It's tomorrow.   (D) It's in the morning.

24. Where can people find their assembly station?
    (A) At home   (B) From the onboard staff
    (C) On the television displays (D) On their keycard

25. When will the drill probably end?
    (A) 2:30 p.m.   (B) 3:00 p.m.   (C) 3:30 p.m.   (D) 4:00 p.m.

Review

A Vocabulary

次の単語の意味を (a)〜(h) から選びなさい。

1. destination (　　) 2. immediately (　　) 3. itinerary (　　) 4. luxury (　　)
5. mandatory (　　) 6. optional (　　) 7. suburbs (　　) 8. tradeshow (　　)

(a) 郊外	(b) 旅行日程	(c) 目的地	(d) 見本市
(e) 選択の	(f) 必須の	(g) 豪華な	(h) すぐに

B Grammar

次の空所に単語を書いて文法・用法を確認しなさい。

受動態

1．受動態：be 動詞＋過去分詞＋ (by)

The hotel is visited by many tourists.（そのホテルには多くの旅行者が訪れます）

The luggage is examined by 1(　　　　　　　) machines at customs.
（荷物は税関でX線の機械によってチェックされます）

2．能動態と受動態の書き換え

{ The travelers easily reached the airport.
{ The airport was easily reached by the travelers.
（旅行者はその空港に簡単に到着しました）

{ I will meet my friend at the airport.
{ My friend will be met by me at the airport.
（私は空港で友人に会うでしょう）

{ Helen is bringing in the carry-on baggage.
{ The carry-on baggage is being brought in by Helen.
（ヘレンは機内手荷物を持ち込んでいます）

3．by 以外の前置詞

Peter Rabbit is known **to** everyone.（ピーターラビットはみんなに知られています）

The old hotel is made **of** 2(　　　　　　).（その古いホテルは木造です）

The runway was covered **with** snow.（滑走路は雪で覆われました）

使役動詞

1．使役動詞 (have, make, let) ＋目的語＋原形不定詞（動詞の原形）

His positive attitude always makes me **feel** good.
（彼の前向きな姿勢はいつも私を気分良くしてくれます）

Please let me **know** the time of 3(　　　　　　　).（到着時刻を教えてください）

2．使役動詞 (get) ＋目的語＋ to 不定詞

I got my mother **to help** me 4(　　　　　　) my travel plans.
（母に私の旅行計画を手伝ってもらいました）

3．使役動詞 (have, get) ＋目的語＋過去分詞

Judy had her suitcase **repaired**.（ジュディはスーツケースを修理してもらいました）

Unit 5　Housing

Check A 26

音声を聞いて英文の空所に単語を書き、適切に描写しているイラストを (A) (B) から選びなさい。

There is a house (　　　　　　) the tall (　　　　　) trees.

(A)　　　　　　　　　　　　　　　　(B)

解答 (　　)

Check B 27

音声を聞いて空所に単語を書き、質問の応答として適切なものを (A) (B) から選びなさい。

Q: You live in an (　　　　　　　), (　　　　　) you?

   (A)　Apartment 3C has new tenants.

   (B)　No, not anymore.　　　　　　　　　　　　解答 (　　)

Check C

次の英文の (　　) の中から適切なものを選びなさい。

1. (There are / There is) a lot of traditional houses in this area.

2. (There are / There is) only one material we can use to repair this kitchen door.

3. This apartment's design is unique, (is it / isn't it)?

4. It would cost a lot to repair this television, (would it / wouldn't it)?

Useful Tips

▶短文穴埋め問題（リーディング Part 1）
・短文穴埋め問題は 15 問です。
・選択肢を見て品詞・文法・用法のうち、何が問われているのかを考えましょう。
・空所に語句を入れて、文法的に正しいか、きちんと意味をなす短文になるかを確認しましょう。
・基礎的な語彙・文法の知識をしっかり身につけておきましょう。
・やさしいビジネス単語も覚えておきましょう。

\<Listening Test\>
Part 1 Four Pictures 28

As you look at the four pictures, listen to the short sentence. Choose the picture that the sentence best describes. Then mark your answer (A), (B), (C), or (D).

1. (A)

(B)

(C)

(D)

Part 2 Question-Response 29

You will hear three questions, each followed by four possible responses. Choose the best response (A), (B), (C), or (D) to each question.

2. (A) Really, can I? (B) None has three bedrooms.
   (C) No, you can't find any near here. (D) I prefer houses.

3. (A) Next week would be better. (B) Yes, and I was very impressed.
   (C) It's more than 100 years old. (D) I'll watch it tomorrow.

4. (A) Very much. (B) I'm considering buying a new one.
   (C) Not really, no. (D) No thank you. Maybe later.

Part 3 Conversations

[A] Questions 5-6 refer to the following conversation.

5. What will they do to the house first?
   - (A) Rebuild it.
   - (B) Repaint the outside.
   - (C) Wallpaper the inside.
   - (D) Wait for the rainy season to end.

6. Why does the woman disagree with the man?
   - (A) It is too cold outside.
   - (B) It's not the right time of year to paint outside.
   - (C) Painting is too expensive.
   - (D) The house doesn't need new paint.

[B] Questions 7-8 refer to the following conversation and notice.

> Payment methods
> 1-bedroom — Cash
> 2-bedroom — Credit card

7. What is the man going to take?
   - (A) He'll decide later.
   - (B) The cheaper one.
   - (C) The one-bedroom apartment.
   - (D) The two-bedroom apartment.

8. Look at the notice. Which payment method will the man have to choose?
   - (A) Any method will do.
   - (B) By credit card.
   - (C) Online.
   - (D) In cash.

Part 4 Talks

[A] Questions 9-10 refer to the following talk.

9. What kind of committee is it?
   - (A) Crime prevention.
   - (B) Neighborhood clean-up.
   - (C) Parking.
   - (D) Rent control.

10. According to the speaker, what is the result?
    - (A) Almost no robbery incidents.
    - (B) The rent hasn't increased.
    - (C) The area is very clean.
    - (D) The area is very quiet.

[B] Questions 11-12 refer to the following talk and notice.

> **House to let**
> A three-bedroom house conveniently located near the city center.
> You can see the house on Tuesdays or Fridays.

11. Who most likely is the man?
    - (A) A carpenter.
    - (B) A real-estate agent.
    - (C) A home buyer.
    - (D) An appliance salesperson.

12. Look at the notice. When will the man take his customer to view this house?
    - (A) This Friday. (B) This Sunday. (C) Next Monday. (D) Next Tuesday.

\<Reading Test\>
Part 1 Sentence Completion

Questions 13-17 are incomplete sentences. Choose the phrase (A), (B), (C), or (D) that best completes each sentence.

13. _____ many people living in this neighborhood in those days.
    (A) There has been
    (B) There is not
    (C) There was not
    (D) There were not

14. _____ many flowers in the garden in front of the house.
    (A) There has been
    (B) There is
    (C) There used to be
    (D) There was

15. _____ a major renovation in this apartment building next month.
    (A) There are
    (B) There was
    (C) There were
    (D) There will be

16. Georgia will move to a new apartment next week, _____?
    (A) does she
    (B) isn't she
    (C) wasn't she
    (D) won't she

17. He can afford to rent this beautiful house, _____?
    (A) can he
    (B) can't he
    (C) does he
    (D) doesn't he

Part 2 Text Completion

There are three numbered blanks (18), (19), and (20) in the short reading passage. Choose the answer (A), (B), (C), or (D) that best fills in the blank and completes the text.

> *TechKnow* makes the fastest computers on the planet. (18)_____ there anything that they haven't made better and faster? *TechKnow*'s new line-up of products will be announced next Monday. There is no (19)_____ what the company will give us this time. (20)_____

18. (A) Is
    (B) Are
    (C) Were
    (D) Would

19. (A) knows
    (B) knew
    (C) knowing
    (D) to know

20. (A) Buy yours today!
    (B) Their business is growing.
    (C) We can hardly wait to find out!
    (D) Why wait until Sunday?

Part 3 Reading Comprehension

Questions 21-22 refer to the following notice.

FOR RENT: Commercial Retail and Office Space
Available Now

Located five blocks from Main Street Station in the heart of the financial district. First floor retail space (462m²), with 4th and 5th floor office space (total 1,006 m²) also available. Three-year fixed contract. Call for rates and rental.

---

21. Who would this space most likely be useful for?

    (A) A bank (B) A sports team (C) A large family (D) A public school

22. How would an interested person arrange to rent the space?

    (A) Go to Main Street Station   (B) Pay $1,006 per square meter

    (C) Telephone the agent   (D) Wait three years for a new contract

Questions 23-25 refer to the following notice.

Build Our Future Green!

"Green" means "good for the environment." "Building green," therefore, means designs and buildings that have a positive impact on the local environment. Building green reduces waste, saves resources, and is sustainable.

Green buildings:
- Are designed by architects and built with safe and sustainable materials.
- Use renewable energy sources.
- Improve water use (collect rain water, reduce water volume in toilets and showers).
- Have plants to beautify the space and clean the air (rooftop gardens, interior planters).

Green buildings improve our quality of life and help keep our planet healthy!
Go green today!

---

23. Why should we "build green"?

    (A) It's easy to do.   (B) It's good for us and the planet.

    (C) It's inexpensive.   (D) It's wasteful.

24. Which of the following would be the best at designing a green building?

    (A) A biologist   (B) A politician   (C) A surgeon   (D) An architect

25. How might the average home owner make the building "green"?

    (A) Design a green building   (B) Have plants in the house

    (C) Live a healthy life   (D) Take a lot of showers

Review

A Vocabulary

次の単語の意味を (a)〜(h) から選びなさい。

1. anniversary (　) 2. architect (　) 3. available (　) 4. electricity (　)

5. environment (　) 6. reduce (　) 7. renovation (　) 8. sustainable (　)

(a) リフォーム	(b) 環境	(c) 記念日	(d) 建築家
(e) 電気	(f) 持続可能な	(g) 利用できる	(h) 減らす

B Grammar

次の空所に単語を書いて文法・用法を確認しなさい。

There 構文

1. **There is [...], There are [...]** の使い方
   ☞ There は形式的な主語で、[...] が意味上の主語
   名詞 [...] が単数形なら There is、名詞 [...] が複数形なら There are

   There is a new **condo** near here.（この近くに新しいマンションがあります）

   There are some nice **apartments** in this area.
   （この地域にはいくつかの良いアパートがあります）

2. **There is / are** の否定文、疑問文、未来形

   There are no apartments 1(　　　　) rent around here.
   （このあたりに賃貸アパートはありません）

   Are there any problems with the condos?（そのマンションに何か問題はありますか）

   There will be an information 2(　　　　　) about the apartments tomorrow.
   （明日、アパートについて情報を提供するセッションがあります）

3. **There is** の慣用表現

   There is no use repairing the house.（家を修理するのは無駄です）

付加疑問文

相手に同意を求めたり、確認したりする疑問文「〜ですよね」
☞ 肯定文では「〜，否定＋（主語を表す）代名詞？」
　否定文では「〜，肯定＋（主語を表す）代名詞？」

1. be 動詞の付加疑問文と答え方 ＜肯定文の場合＞

   The apartment is new, isn't 3(　　　　)?（そのアパートは新しいですよね）
   { Yes, it is.（はい、新しいです）
   { No, it isn't.（いいえ、新しくありません）

2. 一般動詞の付加疑問文と答え方 ＜否定文の場合＞

   He doesn't like the apartment, 4(　　　　) he?
   （彼はそのアパートが気に入っていませんよね）
   { Yes, he does.（いいえ、気に入っています）
   { No, he doesn't.（はい、気に入っていません）

3. 助動詞の付加疑問文と答え方 ＜否定文の場合＞

   You cannot rent an apartment, can you?（アパートを借りられませんよね）
   { Yes, I can.（いいえ、借りられます）
   { No, I can't.（はい、借りられません）

Warm-up

Check A 32

音声を聞いて英文の空所に単語を書き、適切に描写しているイラストを (A)(B) から選びなさい。

They are (　　　　　　) the (　　　　　) uniform.

(A)

(B)

解答 (　　)

Check B 33

音声を聞いて空所に単語を書き、質問の応答として適切なものを (A)(B) から選びなさい。

Q: (　　　　) do you (　　　　　　　) our professor?

   (A) Because I forgot my homework.

   (B) Because she's very enthusiastic.　　　　　解答 (　　)

Check C

次の英文の (　　　) の中から適切なものを選びなさい。

1. Students are allowed to take (a bottle / few) of water into the classroom.

2. My biology teacher gave me an (A grade / advice) in the class.

3. Students can get a (knowledge / library card) from the school.

4. Students often have a bowl of (bread / soup) for lunch in the cafeteria.

Useful Tips

▶長文穴埋め問題（リーディング Part 2）
・長文穴埋め問題数は 15 問あります。
・1 つの長文に 3 つの空所があり、空所に入れる選択肢は語句とセンテンスです。
・解き方は、短文穴埋め問題（Part 1）と基本的に同じです。
・選択肢を見て、語彙、文法、用法の何が問われているのかを考えましょう。
・センテンスを選ぶ問題は、空所の前後の文脈だけでなく、全体の内容を理解して答えましょう。

<Listening Test>
Part 1 Four Pictures 34

As you look at the four pictures, listen to the short sentence. Choose the picture that the sentence best describes. Then mark your answer (A), (B), (C), or (D).

1. (A)    (B)

(C)    (D)

Part 2 Question-Response 35

You will hear three questions, each followed by four possible responses. Choose the best response (A), (B), (C), or (D) to each question.

2. (A) I can make copies for you.　(B) Your report was my favorite.
   (C) I was really busy last week.　(D) Neither did I.

3. (A) The books were moved to another place.
   (B) There is a bookshelf over there.
   (C) I'll fill it for you.
   (D) This dictionary belongs to me.

4. (A) Every day on my smartphone.　(B) Because it's very informative.
   (C) He will change the channel.　(D) This watch isn't new.

Part 3 Conversations 36

[A] Questions 5-6 refer to the following conversation.

5. What did the man do today?
   - (A) Ate his dinner.
   - (B) Finished his homework.
   - (C) Got a 90 on a quiz.
   - (D) Had a math test.

6. What will the man do tomorrow?
   - (A) Have a math test.
   - (B) Have a science test.
   - (C) Get dinner ready.
   - (D) Get started on his homework.

[B] Questions 7-8 refer to the following conversation and notice.

> ### Library Open Hours
> Tuesday through Friday: 9:00 a.m.-7:00 p.m.
> Saturdays, Sundays, and National Holidays: 9:00 a.m.-5:00 p.m.

7. What will the woman do?
   - (A) Come back to the library tomorrow.
   - (B) Get her books at the bookstore.
   - (C) Hurry to the fifth floor.
   - (D) Look up the information on the internet.

8. Look at the notice. When will the woman most likely go to the sixth floor?
   - (A) At 5 p.m. today.
   - (B) At 7 p.m. today.
   - (C) At 7 a.m. tomorrow.
   - (D) At 9 a.m. tomorrow.

Part 4 Talks 37

[A] Questions 9-10 refer to the following talk and schedule.

> | | |
> |---|---|
> | *Mondays:* | *grammar test* |
> | *Tuesdays:* | *vocabulary test* |
> | *Wednesdays:* | *reading test* |
> | *Thursdays:* | *listening test* |

9. What will happen first?
   - (A) A vocabulary test.
   - (B) A presentation contest.
   - (C) Presentation practice time.
   - (D) Today's lecture.

10. Look at the schedule. What day is it today?
    - (A) Monday.
    - (B) Tuesday.
    - (C) Wednesday.
    - (D) Thursday.

[B] Questions 11-12 refer to the following talk.

11. What should students in the library do with books they don't want?
    - (A) Leave them on the table.
    - (B) Place them in the book bin.
    - (C) Replace them on the shelf.
    - (D) Take them to the front desk.

12. When should borrowed books be returned?
    - (A) In ten days.
    - (B) The following day.
    - (C) Two weeks from now.
    - (D) Within a week.

\<Reading Test\>
Part 1 Sentence Completion

Questions 13-17 are incomplete sentences. Choose the word (A), (B), (C), or (D) that best completes each sentence.

13. Students usually take a number of _____ each semester.
    (A) homework (B) learning   (C) subjects   (D) work

14. Students can get necessary _____ in the library.
    (A) book   (B) information   (C) document   (D) item

15. This library features many _____, including audio visual rooms.
    (A) facilities   (B) machines   (C) opportunity   (D) service

16. Two-thirds _____ is necessary to pass this course.
    (A) attend   (B) attended   (C) attending   (D) attendance

17. Only library users have the _____ to use the private reading room.
    (A) ability   (B) reason   (C) right   (D) talent

Part 2 Text Completion

There are three numbered blanks (18), (19), and (20) in the short reading passage. Choose the answer (A), (B), (C), or (D) that best fills in the blank and completes the text.

Classroom Rules

1. Don't eat – but a (18)_____ of your favorite beverage (tea, water, etc.) is okay.
2. Bring a pen and at least three (19)_____ of paper.
3. Be respectful – don't make (20)_____ , tidy up, etc.

18. (A) bottle
    (B) bowl
    (C) lots
    (D) packet

19. (A) piece
    (B) pint
    (C) sheets
    (D) things

20. (A) noise
    (B) noisy
    (C) the noise
    (D) the noises

Part 3 Reading Comprehension

Questions 21-22 refer to the following message.

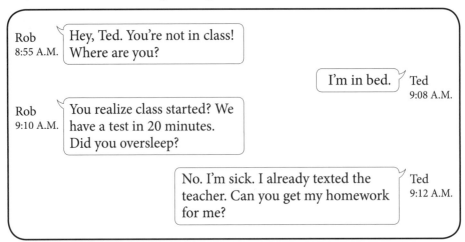

Rob
8:55 A.M. Hey, Ted. You're not in class! Where are you?

I'm in bed. Ted
9:08 A.M.

Rob
9:10 A.M. You realize class started? We have a test in 20 minutes. Did you oversleep?

No. I'm sick. I already texted the teacher. Can you get my homework for me? Ted
9:12 A.M.

21. Which of the following best describes Ted?
(A) He overslept.
(B) He's a teacher.
(C) He's ill.
(D) He's in class.

22. How will Rob help?
(A) Get Ted's assignments
(B) Get Ted's test score
(C) Take Ted's test for him
(D) Leave a message with the teacher

Questions 23-25 refer to the following Journal.

Journal of Teaching English

A weekly publication from English Teachers of America

TOPIC: English Learners Need More Than a Book
It is no surprise that some English learners do not become good English speakers. Why? Because too often students have their heads down in a book and not up talking. Grammar is essential, but real communication needs real practice.

ADVERTISEMENT: Register for the annual ETA Conference November 6th–9th to be held in Denver, Colorado. Its main topic is better teaching methods.

23. How often is the journal published?
(A) Annually   (B) Once a month   (C) Once a week   (D) Twice a year

24. What does the article suggest doing?
(A) Learning more grammar
(B) More speaking practice
(C) Reading more
(D) Using better textbooks

25. Which topic might be heard at the conference?
(A) Better ways to teach
(B) How to create better advertisements
(C) How to register
(D) The history of Denver, Colorado

Review

A Vocabulary

次の語句の意味を (a)～(h) から選びなさい。

1. assignment ( ) 2. conference ( ) 3. deadline ( ) 4. enthusiastic ( )
5. quiz ( ) 6. informative ( ) 7. front desk ( ) 8. tidy up ( )

(a) 締め切り	(b) 受付	(c) 課題	(d) 小テスト
(e) 大会	(f) 熱心な	(g) 有益な	(h) 片付ける

B Grammar

次の空所に単語を書いて文法・用法を確認しなさい。

名詞

1. 数えられる名詞（可算名詞）
   ・普通名詞 (bicycle, desk, room, etc.)
   ☞ 不定冠詞 (a /an)、定冠詞 (the) が付くか、または複数形になります。

   Is 1( ) a **library** nearby?（近くに図書館がありますか）

   Frank brought a **laptop** to class.（フランクは授業にノートパソコンを持ってきました）

   The **dictionaries** on the **shelf** are 2( ) often.
   （棚の上の辞書はよく利用されています）
   ・集合名詞 (audience, family, police, etc.)

   The **family** are all 3( ).（家族はみんな元気です）

   The **police** are visiting the school.（警察はその学校を訪れています）

2. 数えられない名詞（不可算名詞）
   固有名詞 (Spain, Smith, etc.)、物質名詞 (tea, water, etc.)、抽象名詞 (advice, honesty, etc.)
   ☞ baggage, beer, equipment, furniture, health, knowledge, news, truth, etc. は不可算名詞
   　不定冠詞 (a / an) をつけたり複数形にしない

   { × Can you give me some advices about the homework?
   { ○ Can you give me some advice about the homework?
   （宿題についてアドバイスをくれますか）

   { × I have a good news about my test results.
   { ○ I have good news about my test results.
   （テストの結果について良い知らせがあります）

3. 数えられない名詞の数え方

   I am collecting **a bit of** information.（少し情報を集めています）

   I 4( ) **two glasses of** juice for breakfast.（朝食にジュースを2杯飲みました）
   ☞ **a bottle of** wine, **a cup of** coffee, **a pair of** glasses, **a piece of** cake,
   　a pint of milk, **a sheet of** paper, etc.

Unit 7　Health

Check A 38

音声を聞いて英文の空所に単語を書き、適切に描写しているイラストを (A)(B) から選びなさい。

The doctor is (　　　　　) his (　　　　　) in the hospital.

(A)

(B)
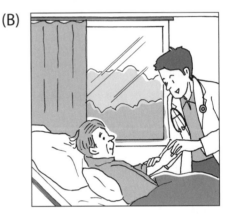

解答（　　）

Check B 39

音声を聞いて空所に単語を書き、応答として適切なものを (A)(B) から選びなさい。

Q: This hospital (　　　　) last (　　　　).
   (A) I heard it has all the latest equipment.
   (B) The man I saw yesterday is a doctor.

解答（　　）

Check C

次の英文の（　　）の中から適切なものを選びなさい。

1. Maria is going to go to (hospitals / the hospital) to see her grandmother.
2. We need to take care of (oneself / ourselves) to keep fit.
3. I find (it / that) difficult to keep up jogging every day.
4. The bed on the right is yours and the one on the left is (my / mine).

Useful Tips

▶読解問題（リーディング Part 3）
・読解問題は 20 問です。
・文書から情報を読み取り、正しく理解する読解力が求められます。
・文書を読む前に設問に目を通し、どんな情報を読み取らなければならないか確認しましょう。
・スキミングで文書の要点をすくい取り、全体の大意を素早く理解しましょう。
・スキャニングで文中から特定の情報がある部分を探し出し、ピンポイントで読みましょう。
・広告やチラシ、メールなどのフォーマットに慣れておきましょう。

Test Questions

<Listening Test>
Part 1 Four Pictures 40

As you look at the four pictures, listen to the short sentence. Choose the picture that the sentence best describes. Then mark your answer (A), (B), (C), or (D).

1. (A)

(B)

(C)

(D)

Part 2 Question-Response 41

You will hear three statements, each followed by four possible responses. Choose the best response (A), (B), (C), or (D) to each statement.

2. (A) I've never seen him before. (B) It's nice to meet you.
   (C) Thank you, I'll go right in. (D) You can buy medicine at a drug store.

3. (A) I sometimes do, too. (B) I'm sort of sick.
   (C) You should stay home. (D) This doctor's office is quite cold.

4. (A) I'll try my best. (B) No, I know the way.
   (C) Only a little. (D) Yes, but I found it.

[A] Questions 5-6 refer to the following conversation.

5. What is probably wrong with the man?
    (A) He has an allergy.   (B) He feels great.
    (C) He has a bad headache.   (D) His medicine isn't working.

6. Where is this conversation most likely taking place?
    (A) At a clinic.   (B) At home.   (C) In an office.   (D) In a classroom.

[B] Questions 7-8 refer to the following conversation and notice.

Maintenance in the Building

Elevator 1 will not be available on Monday the 10th. Please use Elevator 2.
Elevator 2 will not be available on Wednesday the 12th. Please use Elevator 1.

---

7. Where does the woman most likely work?
    (A) A dance studio.   (B) A dentist's office.
    (C) A hair salon.   (D) An emergency room.

8. Look at the notice. Which elevator will the man probably use?
    (A) Either elevator will do.   (B) Elevator 1.
    (C) Elevator 2.   (D) Neither.

[A] Questions 9-10 refer to the following talk.

9. Where most likely is the woman?
    (A) At a clinic.   (B) At a gym.
    (C) In an office.   (D) On a golf course.

10. Who most likely is the woman?
    (A) A fitness instructor.   (B) A hospital patient.
    (C) A police officer.   (D) An elementary school teacher.

[B] Questions 11-12 refer to the following talk and timetable.

9:00- 9:30	Eating healthy
9:30-10:00	Stress management
10:00-10:30	Saving money
10:30-11:00	Q&A

11. What does the man recommend?
    (A) Drinking to relax.   (B) Going to a spa.
    (C) Walking regularly.   (D) Taking a vacation.

12. Look at the timetable. When is this talk most likely taking place?
    (A) 9:00-9:30.   (B) 9:30-10:00.   (C) 10:00-10:30.   (D) 10:30-11:00.

<Reading Test>
Part 1 Sentence Completion

Questions 13-17 are incomplete sentences. Choose the word or phrase (A), (B), (C), or (D) that best completes each sentence.

13. Tracy is looking for _____ to get a medical check-up.
    (A) clinic   (B) a clinic   (C) an clinic   (D) those clinic

14. Dr. Brown is one of _____ doctors in this hospital.
    (A) reliable   (B) reliablest   (C) most reliable   (D) the most reliable

15. I think _____ very important to exercise regularly to stay healthy.
    (A) it's   (B) its   (C) that's   (D) this is

16. When athletes are injured, the team doctor treats _____ .
    (A) they   (B) their   (C) them   (D) themselves

17. On weekends Daniel goes to _____ center that is nearest his house.
    (A) a fitness   (B) fitness   (C) its fitness   (D) the fitness

Part 2 Text Completion

There are three numbered blanks (18), (19), and (20) in the short reading passage. Choose the answer (A), (B), (C), or (D) that best fills in the blank and completes the text.

Dr. Fang Dental Clinic
Appointment Notes

Patient: *Bill Beck*   Date: *May 12*
- *During the cleaning there was* (18)_____ *gum bleeding.*
- *Bill reported a cracked tooth.* (19)_____
- (20)_____ *will not be necessary to repair it.*

---

18. (A) a
    (B) his
    (C) some
    (D) the

19. (A) I didn't want to examine it.
    (B) It was very big.
    (C) The damage was not bad.
    (D) They should be removed.

20. (A) He
    (B) It
    (C) None
    (D) There

Part 3 Reading Comprehension

Questions 21-22 refer to the following notice.

Central Hospital	
4th Floor	Patient Rooms
3rd Floor	Child Specialists
2nd Floor	Ear, Nose, and Throat Specialists
1st Floor	Information, Check-In, Taxi Stand, Bus Stop
B1	Cafeteria, Gift Shop, Pharmacy

21. On which floor would you visit a person who is staying in the hospital?
    (A) 1st floor   (B) 2nd floor   (C) 3rd floor   (D) 4th floor

22. Where do patients get their medicine?
    (A) In the basement   (B) On the 1st floor
    (C) On the 2nd floor   (D) On the 3rd floor

Questions 23-25 refer to the following form.

NEW PATIENT INFORMATION FORM

Name   Billy Bob Thorn   Sex male   Date of birth   09/16/20XX

Occupation construction worker   Height 5'11" Weight   185 lbs

Address   234 Saturn Avenue, Charlestown   Phone   555-3264

MEDICAL HISTORY

Depression	YES (NO)	Low blood pressure	YES (NO)
Headaches	YES (NO)	Smoke or vape	YES (NO)
Heart pains	YES (NO)	Stomachaches	YES (NO)
High blood pressure	YES (NO)	Other	

How often do you exercise? Every day (my job)

How much alcohol do you drink?   2-3 beers on the weekends

What are your symptoms for today's visit? broken ankle? (from a fall at work)

Billy Bob Thorn   _06/12_
Signature   Date

23. Where would this form be used?
    (A) At a police station   (B) At a work site
    (C) In a clinic   (D) In an ambulance

24. Which of these best describes Billy Bob Thorn?
    (A) He is a returning patient.   (B) He is a smoker.
    (C) He is a construction worker.   (D) He is often depressed.

25. Why is Billy Bob Thorn seeking medical help today?
    (A) He has a stomachache.   (B) He isn't feeling well.
    (C) He needs more exercise.   (D) He was injured on the job.

Review

A Vocabulary

次の語句の意味を (a) ～ (h) から選びなさい。

1. headache (　)　　2. pharmacy (　)　　3. sneeze (　)　　4. specialist (　)

5. symptom (　) 6. treat (　) 7. blood pressure (　) 8. medical check-up (　)

(a) 健康診断	(b) 症状	(c) 血圧	(d) 頭痛
(e) 専門医	(f) 薬局	(g) 治療する	(h) くしゃみをする

B Grammar

次の空所に単語を書いて文法・用法を確認しなさい。

冠詞

1. 不定冠詞 a/ an

☞ 初めて話題になる数えられる単数名詞の前に付きます。

Alice is a goalie who 1(　　　　) a uniform.

（アリスはユニフォームを着ているゴールキーパーです）

It is an ad for an expensive fitness club. （それは高級フィットネスクラブの広告です）

2. 定冠詞 the

☞ 可算・不可算、単数・複数を問わず名詞の前につき、特定のものを表します。

The man I saw at the station was a school doctor.

（駅で見かけた男性は学校医でした）

☞ 状況から特定性が明らかな場合

Can you pass the ball to me, please? （ボールを渡してくれますか）

☞ 限定形容詞の最上級

These doctors use the **latest** medical equipment.

（これらの医者は最新の医療機器を使います）

代名詞

1. 人称代名詞：we, my, him, her, mine, yourself など

Paul is a fitness trainer who 2(　　　　) at my gym.

（ポールは私のジムで働くフィットネストレーナーです）

Please do it yourself. （どうぞ自分でしてください）

2. 指示代名詞：this, that, these, those など

This is a new training machine. （これは新しいトレーニングマシンです）

It の用法

1. 天候・日付・時間・距離

It's sunny and hot today. （今日は晴れで暑いです）

It's September 28th today. （今日は9月28日です）

It's 6 p.m. now. （今は午後6時です）

It's about 200 3(　　　　　　) in length. （それは長さが約200メートルです）

2. 形式主語

It is necessary for you to 4(　　　　　) weight. （あなたは体重を減らすことが必要です）

It is certain **that he is in good shape**. （彼の体調が良いのは確かです）

It took me two weeks **to get well**. （良くなるのに2週間かかりました）

It cost him 1,000 dollars **to leave the hospital**.

（彼が退院するのに1,000ドルかかりました）

Shopping

Warm-up

Check A 44

音声を聞いてフレーズの空所に単語を書き、適切に描写しているイラストを (A)(B) から選びなさい。

A woman (　　　　　) at (　　　　　　　) in a clothing store.

(A)

(B)

解答 (　　)

Check B 45

音声を聞いて空所に単語を書き、質問の応答として適切なものを (A)(B) から選びなさい。

Q: (　　　　　) did you (　　　　　) that bag?

   (A) Actually, I bought it online.

   (B) Put it in the bag, please.　　　　　　　　　　　解答 (　　)

Check C

次の英文の (　　) の中から適切なものを選びなさい。

1. Online shopping enables us to purchase goods (easily / easy).

2. This grocery store sells a lot of (freeze / frozen) foods.

3. This supermarket is very popular, because it offers (qualify / quality) products.

4. This department store is (convenient / conveniently) located.

Useful Tips

▶ you の音変化
音変化に音の同化という現象があります。did you は did と you が相互同化して、[dídʒu]「ディヂュ」と、もとの音とは違う、別の音に変わります。

   [t]+[j] → [ʧ]　Didn't you find an apartment?　　　　　[dídnʧu]「ディドンチュ」
   [d]+[j] → [ʤ]　Would you like to live in this condo?　[wúʤu]「ウッヂュ」
   [z]+[j] → [ʒ]　As you know, it is a well-built house.　[əʒú]「アジュ」
   [s]+[j] → [ʃ]　I'll miss you while you are away.　　　[míʃu]「ミシュ」

<Listening Test>
Part 1 Four Pictures   46

As you look at the four pictures, listen to the phrase. Choose the picture that the phrase best describes. Then mark your answer (A), (B), (C), or (D).

1. (A)

(B)

(C)

(D)

Part 2 Question-Response   47

You will hear three questions, each followed by four possible responses. Choose the best response (A), (B), (C), or (D) to each question.

2. (A) After half an hour.
   (C) I borrowed them from Mary.
   (B) At the supermarket.
   (D) He's at the department store.

3. (A) At the box office.
   (C) It's a one-way ticket.
   (B) I see an ATM.
   (D) I'll wait until payday.

4. (A) I can't eat dairy foods.
   (C) In the freezer aisle, over there.
   (B) It doesn't matter.
   (D) You can use a discount coupon.

Part 3 Conversations 🎧 48

[A] Questions 5-6 refer to the following conversation.

5. What does the woman need?

   (A) Aisle two. (B) Groceries. (C) Ketchup. (D) Mayonnaise.

6. Where might this conversation take place?

   (A) At a drugstore. (B) At a supermarket.

   (C) At a restaurant. (D) In a kitchen.

[B] Questions 7-8 refer to the following conversation and floor guide.

4 F	Children's clothes
3 F	Housewares
2 F	Clothes
1 F	Food and cosmetics

7. Which sweater will the woman probably buy?

   (A) The black one. (B) The larger one.

   (C) The small one. (D) The striped one.

8. Look at the floor guide. Which floor are the speakers probably on?

   (A) On the first floor. (B) On the second floor.

   (C) On the third floor. (D) On the fourth floor.

Part 4 Talks 🎧 49

[A] Questions 9-10 refer to the following talk.

9. Which of these can shoppers get a discount on?

   (A) Broccoli. (B) Cereal. (C) Milk. (D) Steak.

10. How much of a discount can shoppers get?

    (A) 5%. (B) 10%. (C) 15%. (D) 30%.

[B] Questions 11-12 refer to the following talk and price list.

A dozen eggs	$3.00
A carton of milk	$2.00
A loaf of bread	$4.00

11. Why does the speaker think Bill is unable to answer his phone?

    (A) He is at the store. (B) He is driving a car.

    (C) His phone is not working properly. (D) He forgot it at home.

12. Look at the price list. How much will Bill pay for the item the woman asks him to pick up?

    (A) $2. (B) $3. (C) $4. (D) $5.

<Reading Test>
Part 1 Sentence Completion
Questions 13-17 are incomplete sentences. Choose the word (A), (B), (C), or (D) that best completes each sentence.

13. You have to be _____ not to buy products that you don't actually need.
    (A) care   (B) careful   (C) carefully   (D) careless

14. This seminar will teach you the _____ skills you need to manage your money well.
    (A) need   (B) necessarily   (C) necessary   (D) necessity

15. Online shopping sites offer a _____ range of items to consumers.
    (A) deep   (B) heavy   (C) long   (D) wide

16. Online shopping can be _____ , since we don't have to go out.
    (A) efficient   (B) friendly   (C) lonely   (D) timely

17. I often buy products online, since I want to get them _____ .
    (A) prompt   (B) quickly   (C) speedy   (D) steady

Part 2 Text Completion
There are three numbered blanks (18), (19), and (20) in the short reading passage. Choose the answer (A), (B), (C), or (D) that best fills in the blank and completes the text.

MY SHOPPING HABITS	
Pros	**Cons**
I'm (18)_____ good at saving money.	Too often, I go shopping because I'm (19)_____ .
I can find good bargains.	I don't need to buy so (20)_____ new things.

18. (A) fair
    (B) fairly
    (C) more fair
    (D) the fairest

19. (A) bored
    (B) boredom
    (C) boring
    (D) boringly

20. (A) enough
    (B) many
    (C) much
    (D) often

Part 3 Reading Comprehension

Questions 21-22 refer to the following advertisement.

For teeth at their very whitest, use Pearl Dental products.

    • Toothpaste   • Mouthwash   • Toothbrushes
    • Dental floss   • Whitening strips

Our toothpaste is scientifically proven to kill germs and whiten teeth. Use twice a day for cleaner teeth and fresher breath. Recommended by 4 out of 5 dentists.

---

21. Why would people use Pearl Dental products?

    (A) For the cleanest home   (B) For the cleanest teeth

    (C) For the healthiest body   (D) For the shiniest hair

22. What is a scientific fact about Pearl Dental toothpaste?

    (A) It can be used twice a day.   (B) It smells fresh.

    (C) It kills germs.   (D) Most dentists recommend it.

Questions 23-25 refer to the following passage.

Gather-Together Farms

Delicious meals delivered directly to you!
We provide fresh local ingredients that you cook yourself!
Register today!

Name _____ Number of eaters _____
Address _____ Email _____

Personalize your menus. (Choose as many as you like.)

Cuisines	Main Dish	Taste	Food Type
Asian	Beef or Pork	Spicy	Low-calorie
Mediterranean	Chicken	Garlicky	Hungry Man
French	Fish or Seafood	Cheesy	Kids Menu
Italian	Vegetarian	No-salt	Healthy

Delivery Days:	M	T	W	Th	F	Sat

---

23. What kind of document is this?

    (A) A comment card   (B) A biography

    (C) A map   (D) A registration form

24. Which of these food types can customers have delivered?

    (A) Children's dishes   (B) Desserts   (C) Fresh Fruit   (D) Mexican

25. On which day is delivery service unavailable?

    (A) Monday   (B) Wednesday   (C) Friday   (D) Sunday

Review

A Vocabulary

次の語句の意味を (a)〜(h) から選びなさい。

1. germ （　） 2. consumer （　） 3. efficient （　） 4. grocery （　）
5. ingredient （　） 6. register （　） 7. flash sale （　） 8. pick up （　）

(a) 材料	(b) 食料品	(c) 細菌	(d) タイムセール
(e) 消費者	(f) 効率的な	(g) 買う	(h) 登録する

B Grammar

次の空所に単語を書いて文法・用法の確認をしなさい。

形容詞

1. 性質形容詞：性質・状態・種類を表す形容詞

Online shopping is convenient these days.
（最近、オンラインショッピングは便利です）

Pamela always wears a nice outfit. （パメラはいつもおしゃれな服を着ています）

I'd like to drink 1(　　　　　　　　　) cold. （何か冷たいものを飲みたいです）

2. 数量形容詞：数・量・程度を表す形容詞

How many times do you go shopping in a week?
（一週間に何回買い物に行きますか）

George has much 2(　　　　　　　　) about online shopping.
（ジョージはオンラインショッピングについて多くの知識があります）

3. 代名形容詞：所有代名詞・指示代名詞・疑問詞を形容詞的に用いたもの

I will explain this supermarket's return policies.
（このスーパーの返品規則を説明します）

Which suit do you like 3(　　　　　　), this one or that one?
（これとあれでは、どちらのスーツがお気に入りですか）

副詞

☞ 動詞・形容詞・副詞・文全体を修飾

John still **remembers** the clerk vividly.
（ジョンはまだその店員をはっきりと覚えています）

Sandra is very **careful** to match her shoes 4(　　　　) her dress.
（サンドラはとても慎重に、靴をドレスに合わせます）

Betty always buys food quite **carefully** at the grocery store.
（ベティは食料品店でいつもかなり慎重に食料品を買います）

Luckily, **this dress fits Julia perfectly**.
（幸運なことに、このドレスはジュリアにピッタリ合います）

Unit 9　Family

Check A 50

音声を聞いて英文の空所に単語を書き、適切に描写しているイラストを (A)(B) から選びなさい。

A family is (　　　　　　) in the (　　　　　　　　).

(A)

(B)

解答 (　　)

Check B 51

応答文を聞いて空所に単語を書き、質問の応答として適切なものを (A)(B) から選びなさい。

Q: (　　　　　　) did your parents (　　　　　　　　) you for your birthday?

 (A) Thank you, that's very kind of you.

 (B) This bicycle, and I love it.　　　　　　　　　　解答 (　　)

Check C

次の英文の (　　) の中から適切なものを選びなさい。

1. Eating with others is (enjoyable / more enjoyable) than eating alone.
2. Recyclable trash should weigh (fewer / less) than three kilograms.
3. We need to recycle (as much / so many) paper as we can.
4. With its seven children, this family is the (larger / largest) in our town.

Useful Tips

▶短縮形
英語の音声的特徴の 1 つに「音の短縮」があります。I'm [aim]「アイム」や I'll [ail]「アイル」など、主語に be 動詞や助動詞が続いたとき、語頭の一部が省略されアポストロフィーをつけて 1 つの語になります。
 They're student volunteers.　[ðer]「ゼァ」(=they are)
 I've been to New York.　[aiv]「アィヴ」(=I have)

\<Listening Test\>
Part 1 Four Pictures 52

As you look at the four pictures, listen to the short sentence. Choose the picture that the sentence best describes. Then mark your answer (A), (B), (C), or (D).

1. (A)

(B)

(C)

(D)

Part 2 Question-Response 53

You will hear three questions, each followed by four possible responses. Choose the best response (A), (B), (C), or (D) to each question.

2. (A) Absolutely not.   (B) Cats, definitely.
   (C) No thanks. I don't want any pets.   (D) Robert has the biggest dog.

3. (A) Actually, both.   (B) It's next Friday afternoon.
   (C) They're coming by car.   (D) They graduated from this university, too.

4. (A) Her husband often comes to this café.
   (B) She's with someone else.
   (C) I'm happy to say that she's my daughter.
   (D) I'm not sure, but she's married.

Part 3 Conversations 🔘 54

[A] Questions 5-6 refer to the following conversation.

5. What sort of pet does the man think his children should get?

   (A) A cat.　　　(B) A dog.　　　(C) A fish.　　　(D) A rabbit.

6. Why does the man suggest getting that kind of pet?

   (A) It is less expensive.　　　(B) It requires less work.

   (C) The children will love it.　　　(D) It is so cute.

[B] Questions 7-8 refer to the following conversation and list.

Bob:	an 18-year-old high-school student
David:	a 21-year-old college student
James:	a 25-year-old office worker
Richard:	a 30-year-old entrepreneur

7. What will the boyfriend do next year?

   (A) Enter college.　　　(B) Change his college major.

   (C) Drop out of college.　　　(D) Graduate from college.

8. Look at the list. Who most likely is Lisa's new boyfriend?

   (A) Bob.　　　(B) David.　　　(C) James.　　　(D) Richard.

Part 4 Talks 🔘 55

[A] Questions 9-10 refer to the following talk.

9. What will the father do at the customer service counter?

   (A) Claim a forgotten bag.　　　(B) Talk to the manager.

   (C) Get his lost son.　　　(D) Buy some blue jeans.

10. Where would you most likely hear this announcement?

   (A) At a department store.　　　(B) At home.

   (C) In an office.　　　(D) In a classroom.

[B] Questions 11-12 refer to the following talk and event board.

Room 1 - 50th wedding anniversary
Room 2 - Business meeting
Room 3 - Wedding reception
Room 4 - Company party

11. Who is the speaker?

   (A) A tour guide.　(B) A wedding guest.　(C) The bride.　(D) The groom.

12. Look at the event board. Where is this speech taking place?

   (A) In Room 1.　(B) In Room 2.　　(C) In Room 3.　　(D) In Room 4.

<Reading Test>
Part 1 Sentence Completion

Questions 13-17 are incomplete sentences. Choose the word or phrase (A), (B), (C), or (D) that best completes each sentence.

13. Newspapers are _____ easier for families to recycle than pet bottles.
    (A) less   (B) many   (C) more   (D) much

14. Some people say the more friends you have, the _____ you will be.
    (A) happier   (B) luckiest   (C) quiet   (D) safety

15. To me, talking with friends is _____ than playing video games.
    (A) exciting   (B) excited   (C) more exciting   (D) most exciting

16. We're going to need a lot of pet food when the big snowstorm comes, so buy _____ you can.
    (A) as much as (B) as many as   (C) more   (D) most

17. To protect the environment, we need to use more _____ products.
    (A) cheaper   (B) eco-friendly (C) expensive   (D) interesting

Part 2 Text Completion

There are three numbered blanks (18), (19), and (20) in the short reading passage. Choose the answer (A), (B), (C), or (D) that best fills in the blank and completes the text.

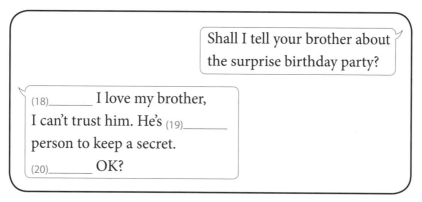

Shall I tell your brother about the surprise birthday party?

(18)_____ I love my brother, I can't trust him. He's (19)_____ person to keep a secret.
(20)_____ OK?

18. (A) Although
    (B) Even more
    (C) However
    (D) Nothing

19. (A) as reliable as
    (B) more reliable
    (C) the reliablest
    (D) the least reliable

20. (A) Don't tell me about it.
    (B) I'll tell him just before the party starts.
    (C) I really like parties.
    (D) The party is next week.

Part 3 Reading Comprehension

Questions 21-22 refer to the following notice.

October is Adopt-a-Pet Month!
Don't shop. Adopt!

Come down to the ANIMAL SERVICES CENTER for cats,
birds, dogs, and rabbits. (Sorry, no turtles!)
Fees for all animals include their shots and GPS-locating microchips.

Come in today to find your new best friend!

1000 Forest Street, Chicago

---

21. Which of these is NOT available?

    (A) Birds   (B) Cats   (C) Dogs   (D) Turtles

22. What do customers NOT have to pay for?

    (A) A cage   (B) A microchip   (C) Shots   (D) An animal

Questions 23-25 refer to the following postcard.

Dear Grandma and Grandpa,

  We've been here in Hawaii for almost 5 days now! 3 more to go! Mom asked me to send this postcard to you to tell you how much we miss you and wish you were here.

  Every day we wake up to sun and sand just outside our hotel window. We went to the Honolulu Zoo and also did some fishing. I tried to surf, but it was harder than I thought.

  I'll call you when we get home.

  Love, Pam

Aug 17th

Mr. and Mrs. Boywid

9876 Wall Street

Springfield, Illinois

---

23. What is the purpose of this postcard?

    (A) To invite someone to Hawaii   (B) To connect with family members

    (C) To reserve a trip to Hawaii   (D) To wish someone a fun holiday

24. Where is their hotel located?

    (A) By the airport   (B) Next to the zoo

    (C) On the beach   (D) Downtown

25. Where will the postcard go?

    (A) To Honolulu   (B) To Pam   (C) To the hotel   (D) To Wall Street

A Vocabulary

次の語句の意味を (a)〜(h) から選びなさい。

1. eco-friendly (　)　2. downtown (　)　3. entrepreneur (　)　4. reliable (　)
5. shot (　)　　6. toast (　)　　7. adopt-a-pet (　)　　8. a steady job (　)

(a) 起業家	(b) 定職	(c) 注射	(d) ペットを引き取る
(e) 都心部に	(f) 環境に優しい	(g) 信頼できる	(h) 乾杯する

B Grammar

次の空所に単語を書いて文法・用法を確認しなさい。

比較表現

1．同等比較：as ＋形容詞・副詞の原級＋ as

Robert is **as** active in sports now **as** when he was in college.
（ロバートは大学生の時と同じぐらい今もスポーツに活発です）

Jenny speaks French **as** well **as** she speaks 1(　　　　　　).
（ジェニーは、スペイン語と同じぐらい上手にフランス語を話します）

2．比較級：比較級＋ than

Phil 2(　　　) care of the family's pets better **than** his sister does.
（フィルは姉よりも上手く家族のペットの世話をします）

My cousin Jack was more helpful **than** I thought he would be.
（いとこのジャックは、私が思っていたよりも役に立ちました）

3．最上級：the ＋最上級

Liz's 3(　　　　) for our family reunion is **the** best of all.
（家族親睦会に関するリズのアイディアはみんなの中で最も良いです）

Nick is **the** 4(　　　　) reliable person of all my friends.
（ニックは私の友人の中で最も信頼できる人です）

比較級・最上級の作り方

	原級	比較級	最上級
＜規則変化＞ ・原級に -er, -est ・語尾が -e は -r, -st ・子音＋ y は y を i にして -er, -est ・短母音＋子音は子音を重ねて -er, -est	fast close easy big	fast**er** clos**er** eas**i**er big**g**er	fast**est** clos**est** eas**i**est big**g**est
2 音節以上の語は more, most / less, least	famous	more famous less famous	most famous least famous
＜不規則変化＞	bad good little	worse better less	worst best least

Unit 10　News

Check A 56

音声を聞いてフレーズの空所に単語を書き、適切に描写しているイラストを (A)(B) から選びなさい。

A woman doing a (　　　　　) broadcast in a (　　　　　).

(A)

(B)

解答 (　　)

Check B 57

会話を聞いて空所に単語を書き、質問に対して適切なものを (A)(B) から選びなさい。

W: Oh no! It just started (　　　　　　　).

M: Maybe we should take a (　　　　　) to the restaurant.

W: Good idea. That's (　　　　　) than getting wet waiting at the bus stop.

　Q: How will they get to the restaurant?

　　(A) By train.　　(B) By car.

解答 (　　)

Check C

次の英文の (　　) の中から適切なものを選びなさい。

1. Emily enjoys (listening / to listen) to podcasts every night.

2. The purpose of this webcast is (report / to report) global weather forecasts.

3. Richard intends (jogging / to jog) even on rainy days.

4. You should avoid (playing / to play) sports in the sun on baking hot days.

Useful Tips

▶動詞「-ed」の発音
　規則動詞の過去・過去分詞形「-ed」の発音のルールを知っておきましょう。

> 動詞の語末の音によります。
> 　有声音→ [d] ：lived [lívd]「リブド」　pulled [púld]「プルド」
> 　無声音→ [t] ：worked [wə́:kt]「ワークト」　looked [lúkt]「ルックト」
> 　[t][d] → [id] ：started [stá:rtid]「スターティド」　ended [éndid]「エンディド」

\<Listening Test\>
Part 1 Four Pictures 58

As you look at the four pictures, listen to the phrase. Choose the picture that the phrase best describes. Then mark your answer (A), (B), (C), or (D).

1. (A)

(B)

(C)

(D)

Part 2 Question-Response 59

You will hear three questions, each followed by four possible responses. Choose the best response (A), (B), (C), or (D) to each question.

2. (A) I can't complain.　　(B) I really hated the thunder.
   (C) OK, I'll think about it.　　(D) It's expected to hit this area tomorrow.

3. (A) I don't know whether to go.
   (B) It comes on at 11.
   (C) Maria hasn't finished her report yet.
   (D) That we should expect freezing temperatures tonight.

4. (A) I don't have one.　　(B) He was checking the news.
   (C) No one was listening to him.　　(D) You can use mine.

Part 3 Conversations　🔘　60

[A] Questions 5-6 refer to the following conversation.

5. What did the man's neighbor do with his garden chairs?
    (A) Borrowed them.　　　　　　(B) Returned them to the man.
    (C) Sold them.　　　　　　　　(D) Threw them away.

6. What is the man worried about next?
    (A) A coming storm.　　　　　　(B) His garden.
    (C) His windows.　　　　　　　(D) The wind and rain.

[B] Questions 7-8 refer to the following conversation and game results.

Cherry Street High School	13 – 3	Blue Line High School
Riverside High School	21 – 7	Waterfront High School

7. How did the man hear about the game?
    (A) From a newspaper.　(B) From Sam.　(C) On TV.　(D) Online.

8. Look at the game results. Which high school does the man support?
    (A) Blue Line High School.　　　(B) Cherry Street High School.
    (C) Riverside High School.　　　(D) Waterfront High School.

Part 4 Talks　🔘　61

[A] Questions 9-10 refer to the following talk.

9. What is the topic of the breaking news broadcast?
    (A) A new office.　　　　　　　(B) A new baby.
    (C) The arrival of spring.　　　(D) A marriage.

10. What will the crown princess do for now?
    (A) Carry out her duties.　　　(B) Go on a overseas trip.
    (C) Take maternity leave.　　　(D) Take sick leave.

[B] Questions 11-12 refer to the following talk and message.

> Hi, Richard. Have you heard the news? Your favorite writer
> has won the Nobel Prize in Literature. I'll have to take your
> advice about reading her work. Jake

11. When were the Nobel Prizes announced?
    (A) By the Nobel Committee.　　　　(B) In Mexico.
    (C) Last night.　　　　　　　　　　(D) This evening.

12. Look at the message. What will Jake most likely do?
    (A) Call Richard and congratulate him.　(B) Go back to work.
    (C) Read Juanita's books.　　　　　　(D) Watch the news.

\<Reading Test\>
Part 1 Sentence Completion

Questions 13-17 are incomplete sentences. Choose the word or phrase (A), (B), (C), or (D) that best completes each sentence.

13. Julia uses her computer _____ the latest news on the internet.
    (A) read   (B) reading   (C) to read   D) was reading

14. These days, I find that it is better _____ to work while listening to the news.
    (A) drive   (B) to drive   (C) driven   (D) driving

15. The traffic report said we need _____ Highway 16 instead of the freeway this afternoon.
    (A) take   (B) took   (C) taken   (D) to take

16. You must live here for at least seven years in order _____ a citizen.
    (A) becoming   (B) for becoming   (C) to become   (D) you becoming

17. _____ about what is happening in world politics is very important.
    (A) Know   (B) Knew   (C) Known   (D) Knowing

Part 2 Text Completion

There are three numbered blanks (18), (19), and (20) in the short reading passage. Choose the answer (A), (B), (C), or (D) that best fills in the blank and completes the text.

Headline News
Crime: *Company employee admits (18)_____ money from her company.*
Local: *Seventy-six-year-old looking forward (19)_____ from high school*
Business: *CEO offers (20)_____ changes in promotion system.*

18. (A) steal
    (B) stealing
    (C) stolen
    (D) to steal

19. (A) graduate
    (B) graduation
    (C) to graduate
    (D) to graduating

20. (A) being made
    (B) making
    (C) of making
    (D) to make

Part 3 Reading Comprehension

Questions 21-22 refer to the following chat.

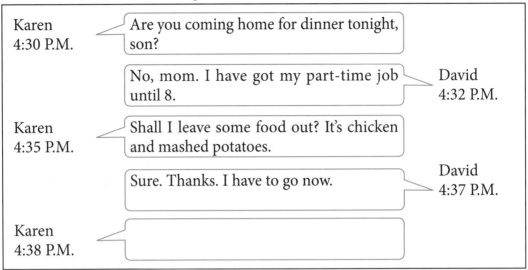

Karen
4:30 P.M.

Are you coming home for dinner tonight, son?

No, mom. I have got my part-time job until 8.

David
4:32 P.M.

Karen
4:35 P.M.

Shall I leave some food out? It's chicken and mashed potatoes.

Sure. Thanks. I have to go now.

David
4:37 P.M.

Karen
4:38 P.M.

21. Why is Karen texting?
    (A) To ask about a part-time job   (B) To check if dinner is needed
    (C) To suggest eating out tonight   (D) To come home by 8:00

22. Which of these would be the best response to David's 4:37 P.M. message?
    (A) "Don't be late for dinner."   (B) "Good night, son."
    (C) "I'll show you how to cook."   (D) "See you around 8:30, then."

Questions 23-25 refer to the following information.

WeatherCenter

Tokyo   **21°C**   **Humidity 67%**   **Clear and sunny**   **Wind 2 kph**

Tomorrow's forecast: High 25°C   Low 21°C   Humidity 70%

Partly cloudy   Light rain   in evening

Get it on your mobile device now!

Download our free WeatherCenter app from the App Shop, or wherever you download your apps. Get up-to-the-minute local and national weather reports, alerts, and radar information for today and tomorrow.

23. What kind of day is it today?
    (A) Cold   (B) Snowy   (C) Stormy   (D) Sunny

24. Which of these is true about tomorrow's weather?
    (A) It will be warmer than today.   (B) It will clear up in the evening.
    (C) It will rain most of the day.   (D) The humidity will be lower.

25. Which of these best describes the WeatherCenter app?
    (A) It can only be downloaded from the App Shop.
    (B) It is quite expensive.
    (C) It specializes in weather forecasts.
    (D) It provides only local information.

A Vocabulary

次の語句の意味を (a)〜(h) から選びなさい。

1. avoid (　)　2. chart (　)　3. forbid (　)　4. forecast (　)　5. freezing (　)
6. breaking news (　)　7. maternity leave (　)　8. up-to-the-minute (　)

(a) ニュース速報	(b) 天気予報	(c) 産休	(d) 図
(e) 最新の	(f) 氷点下の	(g) 避ける	(h) 禁止する

B Grammar

次の空所に単語を書いて文法・用法を確認しなさい。

不定詞と動名詞

1．不定詞：名詞的用法、形容詞的用法、副詞的用法

To go to the moon someday was Tom's biggest dream.
（いつか月に行くことがトムの最大の夢でした）

Sandra has an 1(　　　　　　　　) to hand in today.
（サンドラには今日提出すべき課題があります）

William went to Boston University to study media and communication.
（ウイリアムはメディアとコミュニケーションを学ぶためにボストン大学に行きました）

2．動名詞：動詞の原形に -ing で、主語、補語、目的語、前置詞の目的語の働き

Getting news 2(　　　　) the internet is very efficient.
（インターネットでニュースを入手することはとても効率的です）

Young people love using social media.（若い人はソーシャルメディアを使うのが好きです）

I'm 3(　　　　　　　) forward to voting in the upcoming election.
（来たるべき選挙で投票することを楽しみにしています）

3．不定詞のみを目的語にとる動詞、動名詞のみを目的語にとる動詞

{ 不定詞：afford, agree, claim, decide, plan, refuse, want, wish など
{ 動名詞：avoid, enjoy, deny, finish, give up, mind, miss, resist など

Lillian wants to subscribe to *Time* magazine.
（リリアンは『タイム』誌を定期購読したいと思っています）

Paul has just 4(　　　　　　) reading the news.
（ポールはちょうどニュースを読み終えたところです）

3．不定詞と動名詞で意味が異なる動詞：forget, remember, regret, stop など

{ Alan remembers to check the baseball score every day.
{ （アランは忘れずに毎日野球のスコアを調べています）
{ Alan remembers checking the baseball scores last night.
{ （アランは昨夜野球のスコアを調べたことを覚えています）

Job Hunting

Warm-up

Check A 62

音声を聞いて英文の空所に単語を書き、適切に描写しているイラストを (A)(B) から選びなさい。

The man is wearing a (   ) during a job (   ).

(A)

(B)

解答 (   )

Check B 63

会話を聞いて空所に単語を書き、質問に対して適切なものを (A)(B) から選びなさい。

Man: How (   ) have you worked as a lawyer, Ms. Pope?
Woman: I've worked for six years in Toronto and another (   ) in
             Portland.
Man: That's impressive for your (   ).
   Q: How many places has the woman worked?
     (A) Two.   (B) Nine.   解答 (   )

Check C

次の英文の (   ) の中から適切なものを選びなさい。

1. Interviews will be conducted as scheduled (but / unless) the storm comes.
2. Applicants should be as polite as possible (during / while) the interview.
3. Tom applied for the position (because / while) the salary was very attractive.
4. Contact the personnel department (for / if) you have any questions.

Useful Tips

▶音の弱化
　英語ではストレスのない語は弱く発音されます。接続詞や前置詞は強形と弱形がありますが、
　普通は弱形で発音されます。
　①接続詞 and / or は弱化すると、and は [ən] [n]、or は [ər] [ə] と発音されます。
　　She is energetic and active. [ənǽktiv]「アナクティブ」
　②前置詞は弱く速く発音されます。また語末の子音と次の語頭の母音がつながって、1つの音
　　として聞こえます。
　　Please look at this picture. [lúkə(t)]「ルッア(ト)」

<Listening Test>
Part 1 Four Pictures 64

As you look at the four pictures, listen to the short sentence. Choose the picture that the sentence best describes. Then mark your answer (A), (B), (C), or (D).

1. (A)  (B)

(C)  (D)

Part 2 Question-Response 65

You will hear three questions or statements, each followed by four possible responses. Choose the best response (A), (B), (C), or (D) to each question or statement.

2. (A) I thought she was quite tall, too. (B) Let's start the interview.
   (C) She works very hard. (D) Yes, she had the best resume.

3. (A) I wasn't hired. (B) It lasted half an hour.
   (C) They were behind schedule. (D) Yes, it's my first time.

4. (A) He's an excellent worker. (B) He's been busy lately.
   (C) No, another person got it instead. (D) Yes, he was robbed last night.

Part 3 Conversations 66

[A] Questions 5-6 refer to the following conversation.

5. What is Candidate One lacking?

    (A) Education.   (B) Personality.   (C) Property.   (D) Skills.

6. What does Candidate Two have?

    (A) A better education.   (B) More job experience.

    (C) Communication skills.   (D) Computer skills.

[B] Questions 7-8 refer to the following conversation and message.

> Dear Applicants,
> Please come to our office as planned unless the trains stop running. We are waiting for you.

7. What will probably happen on Thursday?

    (A) Interviews.   (B) A train strike.   (C) A typhoon.   (D) An earthquake.

8. Look at the message. Who most likely sent this message?

    (A) The accounting department.   (B) The marketing department.

    (C) The personnel department.   (D) The public-relations department.

Part 4 Talks 67

[A] Questions 9-10 refer to the following talk.

9. What job is the woman recruiting for?

    (A) Accountant. (B) Salesperson. (C) Secretary.   (D) Technical writer.

10. How should applicants contact the person in charge?

    (A) By email.   (B) By phone.   (C) By regular mail.   (D) In person.

[B] Questions 11-12 refer to the following talk and message.

> Mr. Johnson,
> I am pleased to let you know that you are invited to a one-on-one interview for the position.
> Please come to Room 3 at 10 a.m. next Monday.

11. What is the first step in the hiring process?

    (A) A group interview.   (B) An online application.

    (C) A one-on-one interview.   (D) A written test.

12. Look at the message. What step will Mr. Johnson be at next Monday?

    (A) The first step.   (B) The second step.

    (C) The third step.   (D) The fourth step.

<Reading Test>
Part 1 Sentence Completion

Questions 13-17 are incomplete sentences. Choose the word (A), (B) (C), or (D) that best completes each sentence.

13. _____ putting on his suit, Tim left his house to go to work.

   (A) After   (B) Because   (C) Since   (D) So

14. The Director of Personnel is responsible _____ hiring employees.

   (A) at   (B) for   (C) in   (D) of

15. Mark works in the sales department _____ is one of our best salespeople.

   (A) and   (B) as   (C) but   (D) though

16. The company is now seeking four people _____ advanced computer skills.

   (A) for   (B) of   (C) by   (D) with

17. George went to bed earlier than usual, _____ he has a job interview tomorrow.

   (A) after   (B) because   (C) but   (D) when

Part 2 Text Completion

There are three numbered blanks (18), (19), and (20) in the short reading passage. Choose the answer (A), (B), (C), or (D) that best fills in the blank and completes the text.

To Whom It May Concern,

I am writing because I think I would be a good match (18)_____ your company. Currently, I am a salesclerk at Shoe Land, (19)_____ I am now looking for a management position. (20)_____ This shows that I have excellent people skills.

---

18. (A) about   19. (A) as
   (B) during   (B) but
   (C) for   (C) or
   (D) without   (D) so

20. (A) All my customers say I am very helpful.
   (B) The store is closed today.
   (C) I have never been a manager before.
   (D) I make only 12 dollars an hour.

Part 3 Reading Comprehension

Questions 21-22 refer to the following notice.

Help Wanted

We're an older couple who need a handyman. Tasks would include gardening, lifting and moving some heavier items, maintenance and repairs. Two-three times a week for three-four hours each time. No weekends. $15/hour.

---

21. What does the couple need?

    (A) A job for them to do   (B) A person to help around the house

    (C) Someone to cook their meals   (D) Someone to stay at their house

22. How many times each week do they need the person?

    (A) Only 1   (B) 2-3   (C) 3-4   (D) Only on weekends

Questions 23-25 refer to the following message.

KATE SMITH

Address:
341 Cowell Street
Brighton, California, 87003 USA

Telephone: +1 (541) 555-9510 (Home)
+1 (541) 555-0000 (Cell)
Email: ksmith@wahoo.com

OBJECTIVE: To obtain a position at a travel agency, focusing on customer service and developing leadership skills

EDUCATION:

Bachelor's	Tourism management: Cali University; Los Angeles Sept 2015 – Jul 2019

WORK EXPERIENCE:

Barista	Star Bar: Los Angeles Jan 2018 – Present
Salesclerk	Beyer's Department Store: Brighton Sept 2016 – Dec 2017

RELATED SKILLS:

    Fluent Spanish   Computer   Presentation

---

23. Where does Kate live?

    (A) In Brighton (B) In Boston   (C) In Los Angeles   (D) In Spain

24. What does Kate want to be?

    (A) A barista   (B) A salesclerk (C) A Spanish speaker (D) A travel agent

25. Which of these skills is Kate seeking to improve?

    (A) Computer (B) Presentation   (C) Leadership   (D) Spanish

A Vocabulary

次の語句の意味を (a)～(h) から選びなさい。

1. accountant ( )　　2. candidate ( )　　　　3. employee ( )
4. personality ( )　　5. responsible ( )　　　　6. help wanted ( )
7. in person ( )　　8. personnel department ( )

(a) 直接に	(b) 人事部	(c) 従業員	(d) 会計士
(e) 個性	(f) 応募者	(g) 求人広告	(h) 責任のある

B Grammar

次の空所に単語を書いて文法・用法を確認しなさい。

前置詞

☞ 名詞・代名詞の前に置き、時・場所・理由・方法などを表す

Mason was interviewed for 1(　　　　　) an hour.
（メイソンは 30 分間、面接を受けました）

I arrived at the office in the morning to ask for a job.
（私は仕事を求めるため午前中にオフィスに着きました）

Grace was shortlisted for the position after her interview.
（グレイスは面接の後、そのポジションの最終選考に残りました）

Sophia goes to the company either by bicycle or on 2(　　　　　).
（ソフィアは自転車か徒歩で会社へ行きます）

The personnel of a company are its employees. （企業の人材は社員たちです）

接続詞

☞ 語・句・文をつなぐ

1．等位接続詞：語・句・文を対等に結ぶ（and, but, for, nor, or）

Lucas likes financial affairs and the banking industry.
（ルーカスは金融業と銀行業界が好きです）

Daniel wanted to 3(　　　　　　) his job, but he wasn't able to.
（ダニエルは転職したいと思いましたが、できませんでした）

2．従位接続詞：名詞節を導く（if, that, whether）、副詞節を導く（although, as, because, if, since, until, when, while）

I don't know if Carter will be 4(　　　　　　). ＜名詞節＞
（カーターが昇格するかどうか分かりません）

If she has a job interview today, Mia will get the job. ＜副詞節＞
（もし今日面接を受ければ、ミアは仕事に就けるでしょう）

Unit 12 Advertisements

Warm-up

Check A   68

音声を聞いて英文の空所に単語を書き、適切に描写しているイラストを (A) (B) から選びなさい。

The (   ) is being advertised on (   ).

(A)   (B)

解答 (   )

Check B   69

会話を聞いて空所に単語を書き、質問に対して適切なものを (A) (B) から選びなさい。

Woman: I heard that you are opening a new (   ).
Man: That's right. On 2nd (   ) downtown.
Woman: That will be very convenient for getting (   ) and
           checking my accounts.
    Q: What is opening downtown?
     (A) A bank.   (B) A park.   解答 (   )

Check C

直接話法を間接話法に書き換えるとき、( ) の中から適切なものを選びなさい。

1. { She said, "I am pleased to announce our new product."
   { She said she (is / was) pleased to announce their new product.
2. { My boss said to me, "Create an ad for our new vacuum cleaner."
   { My boss told me (create / to create) an ad for our new vacuum cleaner.
3. { Amy said to me, " When will the store have a sale?"
   { Amy asked me when (the store would / would the store) have a sale.

Useful Tips

▶音変化
音変化の特徴として「音の連結」現象があります。単語の語尾の子音と、後続の単語の母音とがつながって、１つのまとまった音として聞こえます。この現象はナチュラルスピードだけでなく、ゆっくり話す場合でも起こります。
I bought a new product on sale.　[bɔ́ːtə]「ボータ」

Test Questions

<Listening Test>
Part 1 Four Pictures 70

As you look at the four pictures, listen to the short sentence. Choose the picture that the sentence best describes. Then mark your answer (A), (B), (C), or (D).

1. (A)

(B)

(C)

(D)

Part 2 Question-Response 71

You will hear three questions, each followed by four possible responses. Choose the best response (A), (B), (C), or (D) to each question.

2. (A) Let's go ahead with that.
   (C) I'll check on the calendar.
   (B) Let's have lunch at one.
   (D) We should use social media.

3. (A) It's not that old.
   (C) I'll let you know after I try it.
   (B) I prefer something firm.
   (D) It's been a while.

4. (A) It's not that simple.
   (C) I'll try harder next time.
   (B) No, but thanks anyway.
   (D) Yes, it was delicious.

Part 3 Conversations 🔘 72

[A] Questions 5-6 refer to the following conversation.

5. What will the woman buy at the mall?

   (A) Food.　　(B) Clothing.　　(C) Jewelry.　　(D) Luggage.

6. What kind of store will the man probably visit in the mall?

   (A) A clothing store.　　　　(B) A drugstore.
   (C) A grocery store.　　　　(D) An electronics store.

[B] Questions 7-8 refer to the following conversation and schedule.

From 10:00 to 12:00, 30 minutes each	
Bob　　– backpacks	Michael – wallets
Jimmy – briefcases	Nick　　– purses

7. What did the woman find wrong with the man's presentation?

   (A) He didn't ask any questions.　　(B) He wasn't clear enough.
   (C) He didn't explain everything.　　(D) He didn't ask for any feedback.

8. Look at the schedule. Who most likely is the man?

   (A) Bob.　　(B) Jimmy.　　(C) Michael.　　(D) Nick.

Part 4 Talks 🔘 73

[A] Questions 9-10 refer to the following talk.

9. What is the woman selling?

   (A) A children's toy.　　　　(B) A cleaning product.
   (C) A kitchen tool.　　　　(D) A washing machine.

10. Which of these is a good point of this product?

   (A) It can be easily thrown away.　　(B) It can be paid for in installments.
   (C) It can be used for a long time.　　(D) It is very cheap.

[B] Questions 11-12 refer to the following talk and bulletin board.

Room 1 - The accounting department
Room 2 - The sales department
Room 3 - The personnel department
Room 4 - The public-relations department

11. Which holiday will NOT need to be prepared for?

   (A) Christmas.　(B) Halloween.　(C) New Year's Day.　(D) Thanksgiving.

12. Look at the bulletin board. Where is this meeting taking place?

   (A) Room 1.　　(B) Room 2.　　(C) Room 3.　　(D) Room 4.

<Reading Test>
Part 1 Sentence Completion

Questions 13-17 are incomplete sentences. Choose the word or phrase (A), (B), (C), or (D) that best completes each sentence.

13. { Ellie said to me, "I like knitting sweaters by hand."
   { Ellie told me that she _____ knitting sweaters by hand.
   (A) is liking   (B) likes to   (C) liked   (D) was liking

14. { He asked me, "Has the ad helped our sales?"
   { He asked me _____ the ad had helped our sales.
   (A) as   (B) if   (C) that   (D) though

15. { Lucy said to us, "I do ad campaigns using social media."
   { Lucy _____ us that she did ad campaigns using social media.
   (A) say   (B) said   (C) tell   (D) told

16. { Tom said to me, "You should look through the catalog."
   { Tom suggested that I _____ through the catalog.
   (A) look   (B) looks   (C) looking   (D) has looked

17. { He said to me, "You should advertise the item on television."
   { He _____ me to advertise the item on television.
   (A) advised   (B) said   (C) spoke   (D) talked

Part 2 Text Completion

There are three numbered blanks (18), (19), and (20) in the short reading passage. Choose the answer (A), (B), (C), or (D) that best fills in the blank and completes the text.

Kathy,

Today I unpacked the shipment of sweaters, but Bob (18)_____ me that you wanted to do the display. He also said that you (19)_____ do the sales signs. I (20)_____ him to check on the TV ads.

See you on Monday, Jerry

18. (A) said
    (B) say
    (C) tell
    (D) told

19. (A) had
    (B) was
    (C) were
    (D) would

20. (A) advised
    (B) inform
    (C) put
    (D) saw

Part 3 Reading Comprehension

Questions 21-22 refer to the following chart.

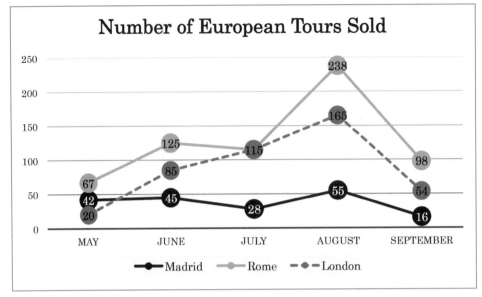

21. Who would most likely be interested in this chart?

(A) A job applicant
(B) A maintenance worker
(C) A receptionist
(D) A sales team

22. What is the most popular tour?

(A) June
(B) London
(C) Madrid
(D) Rome

Questions 23-25 refer to the following email.

From: Jenny Olsen (Vice President)
To: All Product Planning Teams
Date: Tuesday, October 24th
Subject: New product proposals

The deadline for new product designs is October 31st. All teams need to present their new product proposals to the Project Manager, Sandy Wolf, no later than that day.

Proposals will be evaluated by the end of November. The Project Manager will give you feedback by that time. Be prepared to present your proposal to the Board of Directors on December 13th.

Two new products will be chosen for development before the winter vacation.

23. Who will receive this email?

(A) The Board of Directors
(B) Jenny Olsen
(C) Product planners
(D) Sandy Wolf

24. What is the deadline for submitting proposals?
- (A) No later than today
- (B) By the end of November
- (C) December 13th
- (D) The last day of October

25. What will happen last?
- (A) Feedback will be given.
- (B) New products will be selected.
- (C) Proposals will be evaluated.
- (D) The Board will present ideas.

Review

A Vocabulary

次の語句の意味を (a) ～ (h) から選びなさい。

1. account (　) 2. branch (　) 3. development 　(　) 4. durable 　　(　)
5. proposal (　) 6. submit (　) 7. public relations (　) 8. in installments (　)

(a) 開発	(b) 口座	(c) 支店	(d) 企画案
(e) 広報	(f) 分割払いで	(g) 耐久性のある	(h) 提出する

B Grammar

次の空所に単語を書いて文法・用法を確認しなさい。

話法

1. 直接話法と間接話法
☞ 直接話法：話者の発言をそのまま伝える。
　間接話法：人が言ったことを自分の言葉に言い換えて伝える。

She said to me, "**I don't** advertise online."
She told me (that) 1(　　　　) **didn't** advertise online.
（彼女はオンライン広告はしないと私に言いました）

2. 時制の一致
☞ 間接話法で主節の動詞が過去形のときに時制の一致

He said to me, "**I will** purchase a new car."
He told me (that) **he** 2(　　　　) purchase a new car.
（彼は新車を購入すると私に言いました）

3. 命令文、疑問文の話法の書き換え

She said to me, "Put the items on sale."
She told me to put the items on sale.
（彼女は私に商品を売り出すように言いました）

He said to me, "**Do you develop** products? "
He asked me if (whether) 3(　　　　) **developed** products.
（彼は私が製品開発をするかどうか尋ねました）

She said to me, "Who **did** the sales campaign **yesterday**? "
She asked me who **had done** the sales campaign **the day** 4(　　　　　　).
（彼女は昨日、誰が販売キャンペーンをしたかを私に尋ねました）

Unit 13　Office Work

Warm-up

Check A  74

音声を聞いてフレーズの空所に単語を書き、適切に描写しているイラストを (A) (B) から選びなさい。

The two (　　　　) members wearing (　　　　　　) at the office.

(A)

(B)

解答 (　　)

Check B 75

会話を聞いて空所に単語を書き、質問に対して適切なものを (A) (B) から選びなさい。

Man:　　　I'll (　　　　) you up at the airport at 11:30.
Woman:　Great, but I'd like to drop off my bags at the (　　　　) before we go to the office.
Man:　　　No problem. The (　　　　　) doesn't start until 3:00.
　Q: What does the woman want to do first?
　　(A) Go straight to the office.　(B) Stop by her hotel.　　解答 (　　)

Check C

次の各組の文が同じ内容を表すように、空所に適切な語を書きなさい。

1. { You must not forget to hand in a report.
　 { Never (　　　　　) to hand in a report.
2. { The sales trends are very interesting.
　 { (　　　) interesting the sales trends are!
3. { What (　　　) fast copier that is!
　 { How fast (　　　　) copier is!

Useful Tips

▶音の脱落
・音変化の特徴として「音の脱落」現象があります。語末の子音と次の語頭の子音が同じ音の場合、語末の子音が消え1つの音になる現象が起こります。特に同音の破裂音 [p, t, k, b, d, g] が連続するとき、前の語末の子音の音が脱落します。
　He is drinking hot tea to relax.　[hátí:]「ハッティー」
　I want to write a report.　[wántə]「ウァンタ」
・会話では morning [mɔ́ːrniŋ]「モーニン」working [wə́ːrkiŋ]「ワーキン」など、「-ing」の [ŋ] の音が聞こえないことがよくあります。これは無破裂の [ŋ] の音が脱落する現象です。
　She is looking for a knit sweater.　[lúkiŋ]「ルッキン」

\<Listening Test\>
Part 1 Four Pictures 76

As you look at the four pictures, listen to the short sentence. Choose the picture that the phrase best describes. Then mark your answer (A), (B), (C), or (D).

1. (A)   (B)

  (C)   (D)

Part 2 Question-Response 77

You will hear three questions or statements, each followed by four possible responses. Choose the best response (A), (B), (C), or (D) to each question or statement.

2. (A) Great. Have a seat.   (B) I'll check my calendar.
   (C) How have you been?   (D) See you then. Enjoy the conference.

3. (A) I'll order some right away.   (B) No, they're in the top drawer.
   (C) She has a laptop computer.   (D) The copier is out of order.

4. (A) It's on the right, down the hall. (B) It will take longer than expected.
   (C) Of course. What's the address? (D) Supplies are limited.

Part 3 Conversations 78

[A] Questions 5-6 refer to the following conversation and message.

> **Dear Customers,**
>
> To order, go to officeworks.com.
> For over 30 items, call 800-555-1234.

5. What problem did they have?
   (A) The chairs were not available. (B) The man forgot to place the order.
   (C) The tables were out of stock.   (D) No one was in the office.

6. Look at the message. How will they order the items they want?
   (A) At the store.   (B) By phone.   (C) In person.   (D) Online.

[B] Questions 7-8 refer to the following conversation.

7. How did people get a promotion in the past?
   (A) By being a good customer.   (B) By looking good.
   (C) By playing sports with the boss. (D) By making sales.

8. According to the woman, what is the problem with golf?
   (A) It costs too much.   (B) It is too difficult.
   (C) It takes too long.   (D) No one plays these days.

Part 4 Talks 79

[A] Questions 9-10 refer to the following talk.

9. Where is Nathan going next week?
   (A) To a trade fair.   (B) To his office.
   (C) To South Africa.   (D) To South Australia.

10. What will Nathan and the director discuss?
    (A) A new employee.   (B) A new office.
    (C) A new product.   (D) A new director.

[B] Questions 11-12 refer to the following talk and business card.

> **Ms. Terry McCarthy**
> **Director of Marketing**
>
> **Comtex Corporation**
> Phone: 555-3311   Extension: 5120
> 345 Cherry Tree Lane, Boston, MA, USA

11. How many copies did Jane print?
    (A) 12.   (B) 20.   (C) 120.   (D) 200.

12. Look at the business card. What needs to be changed?
    (A) The address.   (B) The company's name.
    (C) The person's name.   (D) The extension number.

<Reading Test>
Part 1 Sentence Completion

Questions 13-17 are incomplete sentences. Choose the word or phrase (A), (B), (C), or (D) that best completes each sentence.

13. What a _____ office desk you have!
    (A) function (B) functions (C) functional (D) functionally

14. _____ careful not to exceed our budget when you order the office furniture.
    (A) Be (B) Been (C) Being (D) To be

15. Kindly _____ us an extra 5% discount since we are ordering over 300 units.
    (A) give (B) gave (C) given (D) giving

16. Rewrite your report by noon, _____ I can hand it in to the office for you.
    (A) and (B) if (C) nor (D) or

17. How _____ you describe the issue!
    (A) accuracy (B) accurate (C) accurately (D) accuse

Part 2 Text Completion

There are three numbered blanks (18), (19), and (20) in the short reading passage. Choose the answer (A), (B), (C), or (D) that best fills in the blank and completes the text.

How to care for your new photocopier.

1. (18)_____ put more than 50 sheets of paper in the document feeder.
2. (19)_____ the Mail Room for refills.
3. Do not use scratchy paper towel to clean the dirty glass! (20)_____

---

18. (A) Nor
    (B) Never
    (C) None
    (D) Not

19. (A) Call
    (B) Call to
    (C) Called
    (D) Calling about

20. (A) Have someone else do it.
    (B) In addition, the glass is already clean.
    (C) Instead, use a soft cloth.
    (D) We don't have enough towels.

Part 3 Reading Comprehension

Questions 21-22 refer to the following schedule.

Paul's Shanghai Tradeshow Schedule

Shanghai Royal Hotel

	Thurs 7th	Fri 8th	Sat 9th	Sun 10th	Mon 11th
Morning			Tradeshow ↓	Tradeshow ↓	Meet Director Wang 10:00
Afternoon	Arrive 2:45 Flight DL 10				Factory tour
Evening	Dinner with colleagues	Opening banquet			Depart 9:52 Flight DL 13

21. What day must Paul check out of his hotel?

    (A) Monday   (B) Tuesday   (C) Saturday   (D) Sunday

22. Which of these will Paul do first after arriving in Shanghai?

    (A) Attend the opening banquet   (B) Dine with his co-workers

    (C) Go to the tradeshow   (D) Take a factory tour

Questions 23-25 refer to the following notice.

Janet and Joan Party Planner

PURCHASE INVOICE

Customer	Selma Kayak & Jon Houston	Email	skyk@wahoo.com
Guests	180	Tables	12

Item	Quantity	Unit Cost	Total Cost
3-layer wedding cake	2	$110	$220
Flower bouquet for each table	12	$65	$780
Bride's flowers (white roses)	1	$142	$142
Champagne	20	$25	$500
Candles	36	$12	$432
TOTAL			$2,074

Delivery Date   June 21st, 1:30 p.m.   Delivery Place   Royal Park Hall

Prepared by
    Joan Jet

Notes
    • *1 lemon cake, 1 chocolate cake*

23. What event is being planned?

    (A) A birthday party   (B) A class reunion

    (C) A company party   (D) A wedding

24. Which item costs the most per unit?

    (A) The bride's flowers   (B) The candles

    (C) The table bouquets   (D) The champagne

25. Which of these is true about this event?
    (A) Half a dozen tables will be used.
    (B) It is being held in the fall.
    (C) Only a few people will be attending.
    (D) There will be two kinds of cake.

Review

A Vocabulary

次の語句の意味を (a) ～ (h) から選びなさい。

1. accurately （　） 2. budget 　　　　　（　） 3. co-worker 　　（　）
4. exceed 　　　（　） 5. functional 　　　　（　） 6. business card （　）
7. out of stock （　） 8. purchase invoice （　）

(a) 予算	(b) 名刺	(c) 同僚	(d) 仕入れ請求書
(e) 在庫切れ	(f) 機能的な	(g) 正確に	(h) 超える

B Grammar

次の空所に単語を書いて文法・用法を確認しなさい。

命令文

　☞ 人に何かを命令・禁止・提案する表現

1．肯定の命令文　動詞の原形＋～「～してください」

Order some office supplies 1(　　　　　) away.（すぐに事務用品を注文してください）

Refill the paper and toner cartridges.（用紙とトナーカートリッジを補充してください）

2．否定の命令文

Don't reduce our office supply 2(　　　　　　　).
（事務用品の予算を減らさないでください）

Never run out of copier paper.（決してコピー用紙を切らしてはいけません）

3．丁寧な命令文

Please deliver these supplies to my office.
（これらの用品をオフィスまで配達してください）

Help 3(　　　　) the office supplies, please.
（オフィス用品を注文するのを手伝ってください）

4．提案の命令文　Let's ＋動詞の原形「～しましょう」

Let's print out a copy of the order 4(　　　　).
（注文書を一部プリントアウトしましょう）

感嘆文

　☞ 驚き、悲しみ、喜びなどの感情を強調して伝える表現

1．感嘆文の形
　　What ＋ (a / an)＋形容詞＋名詞＋主語＋動詞！
　　How ＋形容詞（副詞）＋主語＋動詞！
　　☞名詞があるときは What、名詞がないときは How

2．What と How の書き換え
　　What a good report this is!
　　How good this report is!（これはなんと良い報告書でしょう）

Office Messages

Warm-up

Check A 80

音声を聞いて英文の空所に単語を書き、適切に描写しているイラストを (A) (B) から選びなさい。

The man is (　　　　　) at a message on his (　　　　　　　　).

(A)

(B)

解答 (　　)

Check B 81

トークを聞いて空所に単語を書き、質問に対して適切なものを (A) (B) から選びなさい。

Woman: I'm not in the office right now. Please (　　　　　) a message after
the tone. If the message is (　　　　), please (　　　　) our office
at 555-0000.

Q: What should a person with an emergency message do?
(A) Call the office.　(B) Go to the office.

解答 (　　)

Check C

次の英文の（　）の中から適切なものを選びなさい。

1. The memo was sent to all staff (which / who) work in this company.
2. I want to give the staff some training on the new equipment (that / whose)
they have just received.
3. We'll move into our new office, (which / who) is located downtown.
4. I'd like to know the date (when / where) you first started working here.

Useful Tips

▶音の無声化
・**of course** は [əfkɔ́ːs]「オフコース」と聞こえます。of の [v] は後続する無声子音 [k] の影響を受け、無声化して [f] の音になります。
Of course, he lives alone.　[əfkɔ́ːs]「オフコース」
・**have to** の have [hæv] は後続の to の無声音 [t] の影響を受け、無声化して [hǽftə]「ハフタ」または [hǽftu]「ハフッ」と聞こえます。
I have to go to the country.　[hǽftə]「ハフタ」　[hǽftu]「ハフッ」
▶音の有声化
・無声音 [t] が後ろの母音の音に引きずられて音が濁り、有声音 [d] に変わります。アメリカ英語では「ト」が「ダ」の有声音に変わるのは音の一般的な現象です。
Could you put out the fire?　[púdáu(t)]「プッダゥ(ト)」
What about going to the office?　[(h)wʌ́dəbáu(t)]「ワッダバゥ(ト)」

<Listening Test>
Part 1 Four Pictures 82

As you look at the four pictures, listen to the short sentence. Choose the picture that the sentence best describes. Then mark your answer (A), (B), (C), or (D).

1. (A)

(B)

(C)

(D)

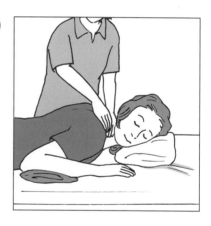

Part 2 Question-Response 83

You will hear three questions, each followed by four possible responses. Choose the best response (A), (B), (C), or (D) to each question.

2. (A) At the tradeshow next week.
   (C) I'll do it.
   (B) I didn't hear the announcement.
   (D) Last spring.

3. (A) I'm sorry, but he's already left.
   (C) No, I'll call back later.
   (B) I already received it.
   (D) Yes, I'll tell her.

4. (A) Are you sure?
   (C) Thanks for your support.
   (B) It's for our new product.
   (D) The memo didn't say.

Part 3 Conversations 84

[A] Questions 5-6 refer to the following conversation.

5. How many more sales do they need to reach their goal?

    (A) 12. (B) 13. (C) 30. (D) 200.

6. Who most likely is the man?

    (A) A buyer. (B) A sales manager. (C) A secretary. (D) An accountant.

[B] Questions 7-8 refer to the following conversation and list.

Report	Staff member
New product project	— Andrew
Market trends	— Jennifer
Sales	— Lily
Online advertising	— Bill

7. What most likely was in the document?

    (A) A new office. (B) Market trends. (C) Next projects. (D) Sales figures.

8. Look at the list. Who is in charge of the document?

    (A) Andrew. (B) Bill. (C) Jennifer. (D) Lily.

Part 4 Talks 85

[A] Questions 9-10 refer to the following talk.

9. What will be closed?

    (A) The café. (B) The factory. (C) The parking lot. (D) The warehouse.

10. How long will it be closed?

    (A) For a whole week. (B) For three weeks.

    (C) For five days. (D) Until further notice.

[B] Questions 11-12 refer to the following talk and notice.

Emergency	Extension
Lights of electricity outage	— 1370
Water or plumbing	— 3510
Sudden illness	— 2560
Other	— 5870

11. What does the man want to save?

    (A) Files and furniture. (B) Expenses. (C) The third floor. (D) A pipe.

12. Look at the notice. Which number should be called?

    (A) 1370. (B) 2560. (C) 3510. (D) 5870.

<Reading Test>
Part 1 Sentence Completion

Questions 13-17 are incomplete sentences. Choose the word (A), (B), (C), or (D) that best completes each sentence.

13. The boss, _____ I'd asked for advice, was pleased with my report.
    (A) when   (B) which   (C) who   (D) whose

14. We will open a new branch office, _____ manager will be Gerald Smith.
    (A) that   (B) who   (C) whose   (D) whom

15. I received a message from the president, _____ I read carefully.
    (A) which   (B) who   (C) whose   (D) whom

16. Customer satisfaction is _____ we focus on.
    (A) that   (B) which   (C) whose   (D) what

17. We will build a new building _____ we can have more work space.
    (A) when   (B) where   (C) which   (D) why

Part 2 Text Completion

There are three numbered blanks (18), (19), and (20) in the short reading passage. Choose the answer (A), (B), (C), or (D) that best fills in the blank and completes the text.

Karen,

Could you please pack my bag for me? I'm being sent to that contract meeting (18)_____ I mentioned before. We're flying at 5:00. The client, (19)_____ plane it is, will take the whole team. I'll need (20)_____ blue travel suit and a silver tie.

18. (A) how
    (B) that
    (C) when
    (D) where

19. (A) that
    (B) what
    (C) which
    (D) whose

20. (A) that
    (B) those
    (C) what
    (D) which

Part 3 Reading Comprehension

Questions 21-22 refer to the following message.

While you're at work, thieves are at work, too!

Help prevent theft in the area.
- Lock your car.
- Leave valuables at home.
- Don't leave things in your car.
- Park near good lighting.
- See something – say something! Call us!

Thanks, from Tower Office Parking Co.

---

21. Who is this message most likely for?

    (A) Car salespeople (B) Mall shoppers

    (C) Office workers (D) Parking lot attendants

22. What should people do if they see a problem?

    (A) Call the police (B) Stay in their car

    (C) Turn on their lights (D) Tell the parking company

Questions 23-25 refer to the following report.

Personnel Committee Meeting Report

On April 21st the Personnel Committee met to discuss a variety of human-resource issues. The main points discussed were as follows:

Promotions: Kayo Ito, part-time data entry staff → full-time (approved)
Slava Petrovich, IT staff → IT team leader (not approved, needs more experience)

Retirements: Marlon Walker (aged 72), requests to retire by end of August
Andrea Newbury (aged 54), requests early retirement (June)

Replacement hires: Two people are needed to replace those retiring. The committee needs to gather resumes as soon as possible. Interviews are planned for the beginning of June.

The Personnel Committee will meet again on May 1st to discuss candidates and further issues.

---

23. What was the purpose of this committee meeting?

    (A) To discuss employee matters

    (B) To decide on contracts with other companies

    (C) To gather more resumes

    (D) To plan future meetings

24. Who will get a promotion?

    (A) Andrea Newbury (B) Kayo Ito (C) Marlon Walker (D) Slava Petrovich

25. When will the job interviews be conducted?

    (A) By April 21st   (B) In early June   (C) In August   (D) On May 1st

Review

A Vocabulary

次の単語の意味を (a)～(h) から選びなさい。

1. committee (　)　2. contract (　)　3. equipment (　)　4. profit (　)
5. resume (　)　6. valuables (　)　7. warehouse (　)　8. human-resource (　)

(a) 貴重品	(b) 利益	(c) 人材の	(d) 履歴書
(e) 契約	(f) 備品	(g) 委員会	(h) 倉庫

B Grammar

次の空所に単語を書いて文法・用法を確認しなさい。

関係詞

１．関係代名詞：接続詞＋代名詞の働き

Karen is the secretary who sends office messages to the staff. ＜主格＞
（カレンは社員にオフィスメッセージを出す秘書です）

I have a friend whose father is a successful entrepreneur. ＜所有格＞
（父親が成功した起業家である友だちがいます）

Ryan was 1(　　　　　　　　) to a new branch in the company that he
works for. ＜目的格＞（ライアンは勤めている会社の新しい支社に転勤しました）

I took a two-week 2(　　　) vacation, which was really relaxing. ＜非制限用法＞
（２週間の有給休暇を取り、本当にくつろげました）

先行詞	主格	所有格	目的格
人	who	whose	whom
物・動物	which	whose	which
人・物・動物	that	―	that

２．関係副詞：接続詞＋副詞の働き（＝前置詞＋関係代名詞）

I 3(　　　　　　　　) the day when I started working at this company. ＜時＞
（この会社で働き始めた日を覚えています）

I visited the research laboratory where Alison works. ＜場所＞
（アリソンが働いている研究所を訪れました）

That is why the boss 4(　　　　　) an office memo every day. ＜理由＞
（それは上司が毎日オフィスメモを送る理由です）

Let me show you how I write professional messages. ＜方法＞
（プロフェッショナルメッセージの書き方をお教えします）

Unit 15　Meetings

Warm-up

Check A 86

音声を聞いて英文の空所に単語を書き、適切に描写しているイラストを (A) (B) から選びなさい。

They are having a (   ) meeting at the (   ).

(A)

(B)

解答 (　　)

Check B 87

トークを聞いて空所に単語を書き、質問に対して適切なものを (A) (B) から選びなさい。

Man: A lot of ocean pollution is (   ) by cigarette filters. Today, I'll be talking about the (   ) that this has on our ecosystem and (   ) to reduce the damage.

Q: Which of these describes the man's talk?

(A) It's about our health.　(B) It's about the environment.　　　解答 (　　)

Check C

次の英文の (　　) の中から適切なものを選びなさい。

1. If I were you, I (will / would) tell Beth that she had better attend the meeting.
2. If we (have / had) had enough time, we could have discussed this matter.
3. (With / Without) your advice, she could not have made such a successful presentation.

Useful Tips

▶目標スコアは？
- ・TOEIC Bridge® L&R Tests は 30〜100 点のスコアで表示されます。85 点なら TOEIC® L&R Test の 470 点に相当します。
- ・TOEIC Bridge® L&R Tests では 85 点以上を目標スコアにしましょう。
- ・英語の基礎力が十分身についたことを確認できる 85 点以上は、総合的な英語力をより一層向上させるベースになります。
- ・85 点以上を取得すれば TOEIC Bridge® L&R Tests から TOEIC® L&R Test へステップアップしましょう。

Test Questions

\<Listening Test\>
Part 1 Four Pictures   88

As you look at the four pictures, listen to the short sentence. Choose the picture that the sentence best describes. Then mark your answer (A), (B), (C), or (D).

1. (A)

(B)

(C)

(D)

Part 2 Question-Response   89

You will hear three questions or statements, each followed by four possible responses. Choose the best response (A), (B), (C), or (D) to each question or statement.

2. (A) Please don't yell.
   (C) No, I'm afraid it's too small to read.
   (B) I'll go get it for you.
   (D) Let's call it a day.

3. (A) He's not available.
   (C) No, he's quite handsome.
   (B) He seldom gets angry.
   (D) Yes, but not with every point.

4. (A) It finished on time.
   (B) Sorry. If I had known the time, I wouldn't have.
   (C) What time does it start?
   (D) Yes, it was canceled.

Part 3 Conversations 90

[A] Questions 5-6 refer to the following conversation.

5. To whom are the man and woman most likely speaking?

   (A) Students.   (B) Hotel guests.   (C) New employees.   (D) Patients.

6. What will happen in the afternoon?

   (A) Computer practice.   (B) Meeting the director.

   (C) More speeches.   (D) Product demonstrations.

[B] Questions 7-8 refer to the following conversation and top page of the proposal.

> ## Proposal [1]
>
> This is a proposal submitted to Johnson [2]
> on Monday, May 21 [3]
> from Mason & Mason, Co.
>
> Written by Nancy Walker
> [4]

7. What has the woman been doing with Johnson?

   (A) Complaining.   (B) Negotiating.   (C) Planning.   (D) Shipping.

8. Look at the top page of the proposal. Where should the woman sign?

   (A) [1].   (B) [2].   (C) [3].   (D) [4].

Part 4 Talks   91

[A] Questions 9-10 refer to the following talk.

9. When did this project start?

   (A) Last week.   (B) Last month.

   (C) Two years ago.   (D) Three years ago.

10. How long is it hoped that this campaign will be used?

    (A) For one month.   (B) For one year.

    (C) For two years.   (D) For three years.

[B] Questions 11-12 refer to the following talk and pass.

> ## Back-stage Pass
>
> Bill Jackson, President of Star Records
> is entitled to enter the area.

11. Who most likely is their client?

    (A) A politician.   (B) A pop star.   (C) An athlete.   (D) An author.

12. Look at the pass. Who is allowed to use it this time?

    (A) Any company employee.   (B) Newly hired employees.

    (C) Security staff.   (D) The company president.

<Reading Test>
Part 1 Sentence Completion

Questions 13-17 are incomplete sentences. Choose the word or phrase (A), (B), (C), or (D) that best completes each sentence.

13. If she had had enough time to get ready, Joanna _____ a successful presentation.
    (A) makes   (B) can make   (C) had made   (D) could have made

14. If I _____ you, I would ask her to update the webpage.
    (A) is   (B) were   (C) could   (D) would

15. _____ your cooperation, we will be able to have a very productive meeting.
    (A) If   (B) Otherwise   (C) With   (D) Without

16. William gives speeches _____ he were a professional speaker.
    (A) as if   (B) because   (C) but for   (D) if only

17. If he had been the chairperson, Tony would _____ yesterday's meeting in two hours.
    (A) conclude   (B) concluded   (C) be concluded   (D) have concluded

Part 2 Text Completion

There are three numbered blanks (18), (19), and (20) in the short reading passage. Choose the answer (A), (B), (C), or (D) that best fills in the blank and completes the text.

> *Doug,*
>
> *Tell the client that if she (18)_____ the price by 10%, we'll negotiate. (19)_____ she doesn't, tell her we will find another supplier to work with. Negotiate with her as if you (20)_____ the CEO.*
>
> *Carrie*

18. (A) reduces
    (B) reduced by
    (C) reducing
    (D) reduction

19. (A) As long as
    (B) Had
    (C) If
    (D) Unless

20. (A) is
    (B) were
    (C) will be
    (D) would be

Part 3 Reading Comprehension

Questions 21-22 refer to the following email.

From: Brook Stone (BStone@wacom.com)
To: Jim Harris (JHarris@wacom.com)
Date: January 15th
Subject: Your paycheck

Hello, Jim,
Unfortunately, we did not receive the information about the number of hours you worked in December in time. We will pay you your regular salary for December this month. However, the 8 hours of overtime you worked in December won't be paid until February.

Brook Stone
Salary and Wages Manager

---

21. What is Brook Stone writing about?

    (A) Jim Harris's salary   (B) Jim's request for time off

    (C) Jim's work performance   (D) Jim's December work schedule

22. When will Jim get his overtime pay?

    (A) In January   (B) In February   (C) In March   (D) In April

Questions 23-25 refer to the following email.

Oceanside Rentals   **July 8th**
5672 Beachwood Drive
Tacoma, Washington 99963

Dear Louise and Bob Brown,

We'd like to thank you for being such valuable customers. Not only have you stayed with us more than 10 times, you have also introduced new guests to our modest facilities. Your kind comments online in the spring about our oceanside vacation rentals attracted many summer vacationers.

Therefore, we would like to offer you two free nights' stay the next time you stay with us. Kindly let us know when you think that will be, and we'll make all the arrangements.

With regards,
Wilma Stanley, Owner

---

23. What type of company is Oceanside Rentals?

    (A) Advertising   (B) Tourism   (C) Social media   (D) Transportation

24. Who is mentioned as a valuable customer?

    (A) Mr. and Mrs. Brown   (B) Tacoma   (C) Oceanside   (D) The owner

25. What will happen the next time the couple stays with Oceanside Rentals?

  (A) They will meet the owner.

  (B) They will make all the arrangements.

  (C) They will get two nights free.

  (D) They will stay for as long as they want.

Review

A Vocabulary

次の単語の意味を (a) ～ (h) から選びなさい。

1. conclude （　） 2. contract （　） 3. cooperation （　） 4. detail （　）

5. entitle 　（　） 6. facility 　（　） 7. negotiate 　　（　） 8. proposal （　）

(a) 施設	(b) 詳細	(c) 契約	(d) 協力
(e) 提案	(f) 交渉する	(g) 終わる	(h) 権利を与える

B Grammar

次の空所に単語を書いて文法・用法を確認しなさい。

仮定法

1．仮定法過去：現在の事実に反することの仮定

　☞ If ＋ S ＋過去形、S ＋ could (would, might, should) ＋動詞の原形

If I knew **the chairperson would allow it, I** would take 1(　　　　　　) in the meeting. （もし議長が許可するのがわかっていれば、会合に参加するでしょう）

If I had **better business skills, I** would get **a pay raise.**

（もしもっと良いビジネス技能があれば、給料が上がるでしょう）

2．仮定法過去完了：過去の事実に反することの仮定

　☞ If ＋ S ＋ had ＋過去分詞、S ＋ could (would, might, should) ＋ have ＋過去分詞

If **she** had 2(　　　　　　) the class, Anna could have learned **some new skills.** （もしアンナが授業に出ていたら、いくつかの新しい技能を学べたでしょう）

If **he** had made **a better presentation, Mike** could have improved **his** 3(　　　　　　).

（もっと良いプレゼンをしていたら、マイクはイメージを高めることができたでしょう）

3．仮定法の慣用的表現

Without **your** 4(　　　　　　), I **couldn't have made** such a speech.

（もしあなたのアドバイスがなければ、そのようなスピーチができなかったでしょう）

Barbara speaks at each meeting as if she **were** a manager.

（バーバラはそれぞれの会議で、まるで経営者であるかのように話します）

Practical TOEIC Bridge® L&R Tests 　　　　　　　　　　[B-908]

TOEIC Bridge® L&R Tests で英語演習

1	刷	2020 年 3 月 30 日
5	刷	2024 年 4 月 10 日

著　者　アリソン　キツマン　　Alison Kitzman

　　　　三原　京　　　　　　　Kei Mihara

　　　　田中　善紀　　　　　　Yoshinori Tanaka

　　　　木村　博是　　　　　　Hiroshi Kimura

発行者　南雲一範　Kazunori Nagumo
発行所　株式会社　南雲堂
　　　　〒162-0801　東京都新宿区山吹町361
　　　　NAN'UN-DO Publishing Co., Ltd.
　　　　361 Yamabuki-cho, Shinjuku-ku, Tokyo 162-0801, Japan
　　　　振替口座：00160-0-46863
　　　　TEL: 03-3268-2311（営業部：学校関係）
　　　　　　　 03-3268-2384（営業部：書店関係）
　　　　　　　 03-3268-2387（編集部）
　　　　FAX: 03-3269-2486

編集者	加藤　敦
組版・印刷	啓文堂
イラスト	パント　大吉
装　丁	Ｎスタジオ
検　印	省　略
コード	ISBN978-4-523-17908-5　　　　C0082

Printed in Japan

落丁・乱丁，その他不良品がございましたら，お取り替えいたします。

E-mail nanundo@post.email.ne.jp
URL https://www.nanun-do.co.jp/